UNCOMMON VALOUR

Sqn. Ldr. A.G. Goulding, DFM

A Goodall paperback
from
Air Data Publications Limited

A Goodall paperback

published by

Air Data Publications Limited
Southside, Manchester Airport,
Wilmslow, Cheshire. SK9 4LL

ACKNOWLEDGEMENTS

This manuscript could not have been written without the help, advice and encouragement of many wartime members of Bomber Command. They are too numerous to mention here; they all know, however, that I am most grateful to each and every one of them.

I would like to express my gratitude to the members of 51 Squadron Association, especially Jim Gill, for their encouragement and assistance. Other individuals who have patiently answered my questions concerning their operational experience, and to whom I am indebted, are Phil Bailey, Jim Feaver, John Maccoss, 'Jack' Ripper, Vic Scott and Ken Staple.

I appreciate the help given by the staff of the Public Records Office, and I owe a debt of gratitude to the staff of Devon County Libraries Dept., Paignton branch: particularly two ladies – Rosemary Brown and Jane Nicholas – who have answered all my cries for help with unfailing charm and courtesy.

Three members of the Women's Auxiliary Air Force I would like to mention are Eileen Morton, Terry Wynyard and the late, and sadly missed, Mary Burch.

The transcript of the broadcast by Sgt. James Ward describing the action for which he was awarded the Victoria Cross is used by kind permission of HM Stationery Office.

My gratitude to Pam Webster, without whose generous help and assistance this manuscript would never have been completed.

Finally, I would like to express my grateful thanks to Air Marshal Sir Harold Martin, KCB, DSO, DFC, AFC, who has always patiently taken time to answer my lengthy correspondence, and whose advice and encouragement are greatly appreciated.

And I must not forget my wife, whose patience, understanding and forbearance are beyond praise.

In this book I have tried to do justice to my former comrades of Bomber Command, whose efforts and achievements have, during the post-war years, sometimes been belittled. This book is a personal viewpoint of Bomber Command's war; any errors of omission and fact are mine, and the responsibility for all opinions expressed is mine and mine alone.

A.G.G.
Torquay, 1985

PROLOGUE

At the outbreak of war in September 1939, Bomber Command had been in existence for little more than three years. The Command came into being on 14 July 1936, with its Headquarters at Uxbridge. The first Commander was Air Chief Marshal Sir John Steed, who was succeeded in September 1937 by Air Chief Marshal Sir Edgar Ludlow-Hewitt.

In July 1936, the Command comprised three groups of regular RAF units, a total of thirty-two squadrons, plus No.6 Group, which consisted of twelve squadrons of the Auxiliary Air Force and Reserve. At the Command's inception, every squadron was without exception equipped with biplane bomber types, but later that year the Air Ministry issued to tender specifications for twin and four-engined monoplane bomber designs for future RAF use.

At first, Bomber Command's expansion and re-equipment with more modern aircraft was relatively slow, but the introduction of more modern designs such as Handley Page Hampdens, Armstrong Whitworth Whitleys, Vickers Wellingtons, Bristol Blenheims and Fairey Battles increased more rapidly as the gathering war clouds mounted. By September 1939, the Command's strength was fifty-three squadrons comprising six groups. Only thirty-three of the squadrons were classified as operational, the remainder being Group Pool (Training) or Reserve units working up to operational status.

The Command's operational strength in Britain was abruptly depleted when, on 2 September 1939, the ten squadrons of Fairey Battles which formed No.1 Group were despatched to France to provide tactical support for the British Expeditionary Force, and No.2 Group's seven Bristol Blenheim squadrons were placed on standby to fly to France as well. This move was, however, postponed and later cancelled.

This reduction of British-based bomber strength meant that Bomber Command at the outbreak of war, 3 September 1939, could call on only twenty-three operational squadrons, approximately 370 aircraft, to mount any sort of bombing offensive against Germany. These units were equipped with Whitleys, Wellingtons, Hampdens and Blenheims; twin-engined medium range aircraft with limited bombload capacities and limited ability to penetrate enemy territory to any significant depth. The aircraft types with which the squadrons were equipped were virtually without any navigational aids, and inadequately armed. None of the aircraft were fitted with self-sealing fuel tanks.

Although the total strength of the Command on 3 September 1939 stood at some 370 aircraft, throughout that September the average daily availability was 280 aircraft. This, then, was the force that Sir Edgar Ludlow-Hewitt commanded on 3 September 1939 and with which he commenced the bombing campaign against Germany; a campaign that was to last for five-and-a-half years. Long, bitter years. Years that saw the Command endure disappointment and tragedy to emerge through success and triumph as the most powerful striking force in British history.

CHAPTER ONE

In the decade immediately preceding the outbreak of the Second World War, the possibility of air bombardment of cities and its attendant horrors became an obsession in Britain and France. In Nazi Germany, of course, free debate had become too eclipsed by propaganda to allow such an obsession to develop. The United States of America alone could view bombing with any detachment, aware that no possible enemy bomber force had the range ever to reach their shores. To the rest of the civilised nations of the world, the vision of aerial bombardment was a horrifying one.

The RAF and Bomber Command stood at the very centre of the public and political debate of this period. The political leaders of the time appeared more concerned with the defence of Britain from air attack than with building up a powerful offensive strike-force capable of taking the attack to the enemy. Some historians have blamed the RAF's senior officers for the woeful state of Bomber Command at the outbreak of hostilities, but in doing this they have been less than just. The blame for Bomber Command's parlous state in September 1939 lay firmly with the politicians and public. Defence spending is never popular with the politician or the public, and it was no more welcome in the 1930s than it is today.

The most celebrated writers of the day attacked the horrors of air attack with a fervour that later generations would bring to bear upon the atomic bomb. *The Times* said in a leader that; 'it would be the bankruptcy of statesmanship to admit that it is a legitimate form of warfare for a nation to destroy its rival capital from the air'. George Bernard Shaw, Beverley Nichols, A.A. Milne and other eminent writers reflected gloomily upon the effects of bombing and denounced its barbarity. The Royal Navy, which still appeared to think that modern warfare could be waged with some sort of medieval chivalry, was foremost in the attack on the RAF and Bomber Command. Admiral of the Fleet Lord Beatty wrote to *The Times*. Admiral Sir Herbert Richmond gave a lecture at the Royal United Services Institution in which he said that 'frightfulness expressly repudiated in sea warfare, appears to be a fundamental principle in the air'. RAF officers, thinking back to the all-out U-boat warfare of 1914–18, and the British Naval blockade of Germany of the First World War were, to put it mildly, rather surprised at this statement.

There was, however, a highly vocal air lobby. The airmen themselves argued repeatedly that, in an age of industrialised slaughter, it was ridiculous to draw an imaginary line at some point between the front line and the cities in which the weapons were manufactured, and to say that the troops who used the weapons were legitimate targets whilst the civilians who made the weapons were not. A body calling itself 'The Hands Off Britain Air Defence League' distributed pamphlets saying, 'Why wait for bombers to leave Berlin at four o'clock and wipe out London at eight? Create a new winged army of long-range British bombers to smash the foreign hornets in their nests!' A Mr J.M. Spaight, a civil servant at the Air Ministry, made a remarkable suggestion in his book *Air Power and Cities*. He suggested that, 'The destruction of property not strictly classifiable as military should be legitimised under strict conditions designed to prevent loss of life, e.g. by confining bombardment of establishments tenanted only by day (as many large factories are) to the hours of darkness'. Mr Spaight appears to have had an amazing faith in the accuracy of aerial bombardment. In fairness, however, it must be admitted that his faith was shared by some of the airmen themselves. Other senior airmen were aware that when war came the main weight of any bomber offensive would inevitably fall upon the enemy cities, the main centres of industrial production, and they were also aware that it would not be possible to ensure that bombs fell only upon the factories and other legitimate military targets. Not surprisingly, however, in view of the prevailing opinion concerning aerial bombardment, these airmen were none too vociferous about their thoughts. The pre-war plans of Bomber Command, and indeed the early war operations undertaken by its aircrews, specified precise targets: shipping, rail-yards, power stations, factories.

It is not possible, however, to accept that the more realistic of the airmen did not understand perfectly well that attack upon an enemy nation would inevitably mean the deaths of civilians. It was, after all, the prospect of destroying the enemy's morale and bringing about the collapse of the enemy's will to resist, that had been the vision of a bomber offensive. This vision would, at that time, have appeared unacceptable to the British public. Indeed, at the height of the bomber offensive in the years 1943–1945, the airmen's political masters were most circumspect in attempting to conceal the true nature of area bombing of enemy cities.

In the 1930s, a time when fierce controversy was raging around the idea of aerial bombardment, when there were attempts to ban the existence of the bomber at international conference tables, it would have been unthinkable for the airmen or their political masters to debate publicly a strategic air offensive in terms of bombing an enemy into suing for peace; this, however, was really the point at issue. The realistic airmen's belief in attacking cities and industrial areas derived not only from realistic analysis of the prospect of destroying enough industrial production plant to wreck the German economy, but also from their belief that the will of the production workers would collapse if enough bombs rained down on their factories and homes.

This concept of a bombing offensive, of course, was hardly likely to receive public or political support in the years immediately preceding the outbreak of war. Both the politicians and public preferred the view that war, if it came, would be fought by the services in front-line engagements, while the civilian heart of the nation would remain divorced from the battles. The flaw with this concept was that it was obsolete. Since the First World War the gulf between fighting man and civilian had ceased to exist. The British naval blockade of that war, which was an attempt to force Germany into surrender by slow starvation of the population, had proved that the civilian population was as much at risk as the fighting man in modern warfare. Despite this, the feeling still persisted that there was something terribly wrong and immoral in bombing attacks on cities and the consequent deaths of civilians. Those airmen who pointed out that the tanks, machine-guns, artillery, etc, which would be used in the front-line engagements, were manufactured in these same cities, were merely being realistic. The same airmen also pointed out that there was no moral distinction between the bombing of cities and industrial regions from the air, and the shelling and siege of cities by armies on the ground; this had been a feature of war down the years.

Despite this, when war came the RAF found that severe restrictions were imposed upon Bomber Command as to the type of objective it could actually attack. No bombs were to be dropped on German soil and, initially, only German naval targets could be attacked. These naval targets, however, did not include dockyards or naval shipping anchored where there was any danger of damage to civilian personnel or property. The reason behind this political indecision and wavering was that, when war broke out, President Roosevelt appealed to all belligerent countries not to engage in unrestricted bombing. France was eager to accede to this request and asked Britain not to bomb any German land targets. France was afraid of retaliation by the Luftwaffe and quite correctly considered she was more likely than Britain to suffer retaliation. Britain, pleased to have more time to build up her forces, agreed to both requests.

Nevertheless Sir Edgar Ludlow-Hewitt did send his bombers over Germany on the first night of the war, 3/4 September, when ten Whitley aircraft of No.4 Group bombed Hamburg, Bremen and part of the industrial Ruhr Valley – with six million propaganda leaflets!

CHAPTER TWO

B omber Command's first offensive bombing action of the Second World War took place on 4 September 1939, approximately twenty-four hours after war was declared. In mid-afternoon fifteen Blenheims of No.2 Group and fourteen Wellingtons of No.3 Group took off to attack German warships reported by reconnaissance aircraft to be in the Schillig Roads and Wilhelmshaven, and off Brunsbüttelkoog.

The attack developed into a near disaster. Flying in rain and low cloud, ten of the aircraft failed to locate the targets and returned to base. Three more aircraft approached British warships but turned away when the vessels displayed the colours of the day. These aircraft also failed to find their targets and returned without bombing. One aircraft dropped bombs on the Danish town of Esbjerg, an error in navigation of some 110 miles. Britain paid compensation and apologised to the neutral Danes for the resultant deaths and damage.

Forced by the rain and low cloud to fly at less than 500 feet, the remaining fifteen aircraft attempted, with great courage, to attack their allotted targets, but were heavily engaged by anti-aircraft fire for which they were an easy target at that low height. The battleship *Admiral Scheer* was hit by at least three bombs, which failed to detonate; other hits on the cruiser *Emden* caused little damage. Five Blenheims and two Wellingtons were shot down. Six of these aircraft were lost to anti-aircraft fire, but one Wellington was shot down by a Messerschmitt Bf 109, the first RAF aircraft shot down by the Luftwaffe in the Second World War.

The Operational Record Book at Bomber Command Headquarters reads, 'An eye-witness account obtained from secret sources shows that the action by the Blenheims was a most gallant affair and according with the best traditions of the Royal Air Force'. This was certainly true; the crews that had located their targets had pressed home their attacks in a most courageous manner at extremely low level. Half the force despatched, however, had failed to find a daylight target approximately 270 miles from the British coast, and of those crews which did find their target, half again had been lost. It was, to say the very least, a disappointing start to Bomber Command's war.

The Command persisted with the policy of sending Wellingtons and Blenheims on daylight sorties in the hope of finding and hitting German naval units, these sorties were termed 'armed reconnaissance'. Whitleys and Hampdens were not sent on these daylight sorties but were used instead on the leaflet-dropping operations at night. The reason for this decision was simple; the Whitleys and Hampdens were totally inadequate in armament to be considered for use over or near enemy territory in daylight.

On 29 September five Hampdens were among several units despatched to the northern coast of Germany where warships had been sighted. This flight of five aircraft from 144 Squadron vanished without trace. The Air Ministry believed then that the loss of these aircraft was due to the weather conditions in the area at the time. The German claim that the Hampdens had all been destroyed by fighters was at first dismissed as propaganda. The truth was that the aircraft had indeed been caught by Bf 109 fighters which had made short work of the Hampdens.

These daylight operations had been undertaken under the theory of the 'self-defending' bomber formation. The Air Staff had firmly embraced this theory – which actually dated back to the First World War. The theory was quite simple; a well-flown formation of bombers should be able to bring sufficient fire power to bear from its own guns to deter enemy fighter attacks and thereby obviate the need for long-range fighter escort as protection. There was only one problem – when put into practice the theory did not work! This was to be

proved disastrously and tragically by the massacre of the
Wellington bombers near Heligoland on 18 December 1939 –
a disaster that was to have far-reaching effects on Bomber
Command and its strategy for the rest of the war.

Throughout October and November 1939 the air war over
the North Sea had been left largely to the aircraft of Coastal
Command. The War Cabinet, however, whilst still expressly
forbidding the bombing of the German mainland, were
anxious to obtain some result to place before the British
public; hopefully the sinking of a German capital ship. With
this in mind, a stepping up of aerial activity against German
naval shipping was prepared. During November several
Wellington squadrons undertook intensive practice attacks
against warships in Belfast Lough, Northern Ireland. The first
operation against German naval vessels was undertaken on 3
December. At 07·00 hours that day three Wellingtons from 38
Squadron, nine from 115 Squadron and twelve from 149
Squadron took off for an armed reconnaissance over the
Heligoland area. Over England the aircraft formed up into
four battle formations of six aircraft each and set course over
the East Anglian coast. They flew north-east, and on reaching
a point to the north of Heligoland the formations turned south,
nearing the island at 11·45 and sighting warships at anchor.

The German defences had detected the Wellingtons
during their approach, and four Bf 109Ds were sent up to
intercept them. The bombers flew on, coming under heavy
anti-aircraft fire from the batteries on the island and the
warships at anchor, and dropped their bombs from 10,000
feet. The bombers claimed hits on a cruiser and a trawler, and
a minesweeper was claimed as sunk. The German trawler
M1407 was in fact hit and subsequently sank. Little other
damage was caused to the targets, but one stick of bombs
dropped around an anti-aircraft battery causing some damage.

The Luftwaffe fighters were too late to prevent the
Wellingtons from releasing their bombs, but intercepted them
as they were withdrawing from the target area. Two fighters

attacked from above and a second pair from below, but were successfully fought off by the Wellington gunners, several of whom were now using the Frazer-Nash power-operated turrets, a feature of the recently delivered Wellington la, which was also fitted with a Frazer-Nash two gun mid-under turret. Two Wellingtons were damaged in the attack and one German fighter was shot down, the pilot later being rescued from the sea. The three remaining fighters, running low on fuel, broke off the engagement and returned to their base.

This action engendered a sense of optimism, completely false, in Bomber Command, since it now appeared that the 'self-defending' bomber theory was well founded. Unfortunately for Bomber Command's hopes, their opponents on 3 December had been flying the Bf 109D, the performance of which was inferior to that of the Bf 109E then coming into service with the Luftwaffe. The 'D' was equipped with rifle calibre machine-guns, and indeed with only half the number of these guns compared with the British Hurricane and Spitfire. How the Wellington would stand up to the Bf 109E or the twin engined Bf 110, both equipped with cannon, was yet to be determined.

With the experience gained from the seemingly successful operation of 3 December, Headquarters Bomber Command scanned the daily reconnaissance reports, impatiently awaiting another opportunity to attack German warships. The opportunity was not long in coming: early in the morning of 14 December a reconnaissance report indicated the presence of German warships in the Heligoland area. Twelve Wellingtons of 99 Squadron were immediately made ready for action. At approximately 11·45 these aircraft took off from their base; the Wellingtons flew in a battle formation of four 'vics', one behind the other.

The squadron's Commanding Officer, Wing Commander J.F. Griffiths DFC, flew in the leading aircraft, from which he would direct the attack. The Wellingtons flew steadily east, arriving in the assigned search area and searching until 14·25 when enemy vessels were sighted steaming south. The ships were identified as a battle cruiser, a cruiser and escorting destroyers. The squadron turned north, then turned through 180 degrees to approach the ships from the rear. At this moment the ships opened fire, all of them putting up a heavy barrage of anti-aircraft fire. As the Wellingtons approached the ships German fighters had taken off to intercept. This time the fighters were Bf 109Es together with Bf 110s. The first three Bf 109Es opened fire at approximately 14·36, and thereafter section after section of Bf 109Es and Bf 110s attacked at intervals of two or three minutes, concentrating on the rear of the formation.

The air battle lasted for a little over twenty minutes, at the end of which time five Wellingtons had been shot down in flames. Wing Commander Griffiths and his remaining crews gave up their attempt to attack the enemy ships, and headed for their base at Newmarket. A sixth Wellington had been badly damaged and crashed in a field near Newmarket, killing the pilot and badly injuring most of the crew. One Bf 110 was shot down into the sea by the leading Wellington's rear-gunner.

Bomber Command's debriefing of the surviving crews led to a complete misunderstanding of the happenings over the Heligoland Bight. During the battle there was undoubtedly confusion among the Wellington crews, understandably so, and some crew members had mistaken Wellingtons going down in flames for twin-engined enemy fighters. The Command conclusion, following the crews' debriefing, was that the shot down Wellingtons had fallen victim to the intense anti-aircraft fire from the ships. The Wellington gunners claimed two Bf 109Es and a Bf 110 destroyed, with a further Bf 109 probably destroyed. Air Vice-Marshal Bottomley, Senior Air Staff Officer, Bomber Command summarised, 'It is by no means certain that enemy fighters did, in fact, succeed in shooting down any of the Wellingtons'. The Command actually thought that, despite heavy losses to anti-aircraft fire, they had scored a victory over the Luftwaffe fighters.

Following the sorties of 5 December and 14 December, a further armed reconnaissance was mounted on 18 December. At 10·00 hours twenty-four Wellingtons took off, nine from No.9 Squadron, six from 37 Squadron and nine from 149 Squadron. The formation was led by Wing Commander Kellett, Commanding Officer of 149 Squadron. The aircraft formed into four units, each of six aircraft, and set course across the North Sea for the Heligoland area. Over the North Sea two of the aircraft turned for home, leaving twenty-two Wellingtons in the formation.

The British aircraft reached the enemy coast at 12·10 without sighting any enemy fighters. Anti-aircraft fire opened up as the bombers passed Bremerhaven but without effect. South of Bremerhaven the Wellingtons turned toward Wilhelmshaven; here they veered north-north-east over the western side of the bay before carrying out a triangular search, passing over the shipyards and the Schillig Roads, and passing Wilhelmshaven on their left side for the second time. At this point shore batteries, together with gunners on the battle cruisers *Scharnhorst* and *Gneisenau,* opened fire without result, until the bombers passed out of range, heading toward the Frisian Islands.

It was as the bombers reached the Frisian Islands that they were engaged by the first of the Luftwaffe fighters. Some Bf 110s were in the air patrolling the Frisians and these were the first fighters to attack; meanwhile, other fighter units were being ordered into the air. It was about 12·30 that the first combat took place and a savage air battle then ensued. For the next thirty-five minutes the Wellingtons were under constant attack from Bf 109Es and Bf 110s. At the end of this time eleven of the Wellingtons had been shot down. A further Wellington was so severely hit it was forced to ditch in the North Sea on the way home, the crew was picked up by a British trawler with the exception of the unfortunate rear-gunner, who was drowned. Six more aircraft were so badly damaged that they either crashed or crash-landed in England. Of the five surviving aircraft, nearly all had sustained some damage. The German losses were three Bf 109s, with one Bf 109E badly damaged. A further eleven German aircraft suffered slight damage.

The battle was a disaster of the greatest magnitude for Bomber Command, although for public consumption the popular press quickly fabricated it into a victory. Senior officers at Headquarters, Bomber Command, were staggered by the losses (incidentally, so were the remaining Wellington crews of No.3 Group), and realised that there would have to be much further consideration given to the 'self-defending' bomber formation theory. Orders were issued for the discontinuance of these armed reconnaissances. Orders were also issued for the bombers to be fitted with self-sealing fuel tanks; consideration was given to increasing the armour of the aircraft and another deficiency noted was that the defensive armament was not good enough.

The tragedy over the Heligoland Bight gave rise both at Air Ministry and HQ Bomber Command to serious concern as to whether, in fact, the Command could continue to operate at all in daylight; no force could afford to take losses on this scale. Although desultory daylight operations still continued for a time, following further grievous losses in similar circumstances during the early days of the Norwegian campaign, British daylight bombing was brought to a halt almost completely.

Incidentally, these terrible losses were suffered during the period referred to by the popular press as the 'phoney war' and were little reported at the time. It is doubtful whether the Wellington crews of No.3 Group thought there was anything phoney about their particular war.

CHAPTER THREE

On 4 April 1940 Sir Edgar Ludlow-Hewitt was replaced as Commander in Chief, Bomber Command, by Sir Charles Portal. Sir Edgar has received a certain amount of scorn and criticism from some historians concerning his period of command. Most of the criticism has been unjustified; Sir Edgar was a highly respected and able commander. With an outstanding record of gallantry and distinguished service to his country, it was Sir Edgar's misfortune to find himself in command of a totally inadequate and ill-equipped force at the outbreak of war. During the first autumn and winter of the war, he proved to be too much of a realist for both those in authority over him in Whitehall and his political masters. Although it was recognised policy that, at the outbreak of war, the RAF should keep twenty-two of its bomber squadrons to provide a reserve training pool, the resulting reduction of the available front-line bombing force appeared to come as something of a shock in political quarters. Then, again in accordance with previously agreed and authorised planning, the ten Battle squadrons of No.1 Group had been ordered to France on 2 September 1939 to form the Advanced Air Striking Force. This, of course, meant that these squadrons were lost to Bomber Command; when war commenced on 3 September the Command's front-line strength had been reduced to twenty-three squadrons. All this was officially approved policy, previously authorised by Cabinet; nevertheless the politicians still appeared surprised by the reduction in the Command's available front-line strength.

When Ludlow-Hewitt confirmed in practice what he had feared beforehand, that he could not venture his force near Germany in daylight without grievous loss, and then insisted on a lengthening of the training courses together with an assignment of the best current types of aircraft to the Operational Training Units to improve efficiency at night, eyebrows were raised in high places.

There was even more consternation when Sir Edgar pointed out that, judged by experience thus far, it would be impossible to carry out without appalling losses the Air Staff's plan (when the War Cabinet withdrew its ban on bombing German land targets) to undertake a full-scale attack by day on industrial and communications targets in the Ruhr. It was this percipience, persistence and realism which undoubtedly caused his replacement. Like many military commanders before him, Sir Edgar had been expected to 'make bricks without straw', and when this had proved impracticable, those in authority decided that the commander must be the scapegoat.

Doubtless inspired by the belief that the post called for someone younger and more optimistic in outlook, the Secretary of State for Air and the Chief of Air Staff looked to Sir Charles Portal. Portal's ability was recognised by everyone in a position to judge, and his work as Air Member for Personnel, in which post he was one of the main architects of the Empire Air Training Scheme, had earned high praise; so on 4 April 1940 Portal arrived at HQ Bomber Command, High Wycombe, to take up his duties as Commander in Chief. The force that Portal took over from Ludlow-Hewitt consisted on April 4 of twenty-four squadrons. Nine of these – the seven Blenheim squadrons of No.2 Group and two Whitley squadrons of No.4 Group – were selected to collaborate with the armies if the Germans attacked France or the Low Countries. This left fifteen squadrons of Wellingtons, Whitleys and Hampdens to carry out any bombing offensive against Germany. This strategic bomber force totalled some 240 aircraft, of which only about two-thirds would normally be fully serviceable and available for operational duty.

Portal, therefore, entered upon his period of command

with an even smaller force than that with which Bomber Command initially went to war on 3 September 1939. The force was small in number, but the aircrews were in good heart, and Portal inherited some excellent subordinates. At High Wycombe the Senior Air Staff Officer was Bottomley, later to be Deputy Chief of Air Staff. The Group Commanders included Arthur Coningham, later to achieve fame with the Tactical Air Forces, and Arthur Harris, who would become Bomber Command's commander for the full-scale bombing assault on Germany.

The new commander had been in charge at High Wycombe less than a week when, early on 9 April 1940, Germany invaded Norway and Denmark. On 7 April, a force of Blenheims sent out to attack a large German naval force in the Kattegat did no damage to the ships, but brought back valuable information on the course and composition of the convoy. Other reports were received at the same time which led the Royal Navy to the false conclusion that the enemy warships intended breaking out into the Atlantic trade routes. Early on 9 April, with this good luck and the weather in their favour, the Germans seized the principal ports of Norway. On 10 April, thanks to excellent air support, the enemy had possession of all the main airfields. During the same period the Germans occupied Denmark to safeguard their lines of communication.

Bomber Command's participation in the Norwegian campaign took two main forms. At first the chief task of the Command was to seek out and attack enemy warships, together with supply ships. These operations met with little success, and when twelve Hampdens attempted to attack a warship at Kristiansand, the Command learnt once again the hard way that unescorted bombers were no match for the Luftwaffe's fighters. The Hampdens had no armament capable of dealing with a beam attack and were shot down from the wingman inwards until only six survived. This disaster only confirmed, if further confirmation were needed, the lessons of September and December 1939.

Another method of attacking enemy shipping, and one on which Portal was very much keener, was dropping mines in the enemy's sea lanes. This type of operation, known by the code name 'gardening', was carried out along the whole length of the German sea lanes to Norway. Arthur Harris's Hampdens did the bulk of the minelaying, and a total of some 300 mines were dropped during the moon periods of April and May. Eleven aircraft were lost on these minelaying operations but the enemy losses were twelve vessels, totalling some 18,000 tons. The minelaying, together with British submarine activity, forced the Germans to give up using the longer sea routes to Norway and concentrate on the short passage from Jutland. Portal and Harris were not, of course, aware of these successes in detail, but from the start of the operations they were certain of their value. For the rest of the war both men maintained a great faith in minelaying, and the final reckoning fully justified this faith.

Bomber Command's second task was to attempt to restrict enemy air activity in Norway. If Britain were to be successful with forces landed at Aandalsnes and Namsos, and if they were to be successful in recovering Narvik, which Britain hoped to do, it would be necessary to hold in check 600 or so German bombers, fighters and reconnaissance aircraft which were at present dominant in the Norwegian skies. Incredibly, the main burden of this task fell on Portal's England-based bombers. Without firmly held positions and without any available landing strips the Allied troops could expect very little support from fighters except in the Narvik area; the ground troops were also lacking in anti-aircraft guns. It therefore depended largely on Bomber Command to reduce the effectiveness of the enemy air arm.

Portal made every effort to do so. This meant attacking the airfields in Norway and Denmark from which enemy aircraft were operating. The airfields in Northern Germany could not be bombed since the political orders were that no land targets in Germany were to be attacked. Portal had serious reservations about the bombing of distant airfields. It was one thing for fighters to sweep in, take the enemy by surprise and shoot up his airfield. This sort of operation could be a profitable one, if the airfield were near enough to be taken by surprise. It was a different matter, however, to attempt to attack airfields across the whole width of the North Sea. To attack at night, when the targets would be difficult to find, promised little in the way of results; and to attempt to attack in daylight, when there might be no cloud cover at the critical time, promised some occasions when the attackers' losses would far outweigh their achievements. Bomber Command had to attempt the task, for there was no other way to try to restrict the enemy air activity which was playing such a large part in the German success.

The first attack, which was the first to be carried out on a mainland target by British aircraft during the Second World War, was made against Stavanger airfield on the night of 11/12 April. This airfield, approximately 450 miles away, was the nearest to Bomber Command's bases. From then on six or more bombers raided airfields in Norway and Denmark practically every day and night through April into May. The principal target was Stavanger, but attacks were made on airfields as distant as Vaernes (some 750 miles from the bases), Oslo, Kristiansand and Aalborg in Denmark.

The difficulties under which the crews carried out these operations were enormous. There was the difficulty of attacking airfields at extreme range during the shortening nights, or during daylight in the face of the enemy fighters in vastly superior numbers. The crews had to fly over great stretches of sea, often in appalling weather, with the bare minimum of navigational equipment, using poor maps and charts of the area they were to attack. No preparations had been made for any attack on Norway and, incredible as it seems now, urban identification on some raids depended on town maps torn from the pages of Baedekers. It was extremely difficult to establish what damage their bombing was inflicting, night photography at that time was nowhere near as sophisticated as it was to become later in the war.

On 24 April Commander in Chief Portal actually wrote to the Vice Chief of the Air Staff, Air Marshal Sir Richard Pierse, asking whether the Air Staff could provide him with information about the effect of his own command's operations. Portal wanted to know whether the minelaying was having any effect, were the attacks on the airfields effective and, above all, could the Photographic Reconnaissance Unit (under the direct control of the Air Ministry) be sent over the targets to obtain more detailed information on the airfields. At this stage of the operations the commander was as much in the dark as his crews. Whatever effect the raids were having it was not sufficient to maintain resistance in Central Norway, but an intensive effort during the evacuation from that area did help the Allied troops to make their escape.

Portal was also facing another difficulty; though ordered to give powerful support to the troops in Norway he was also expected by the Air Staff to preserve his full strength for the greater struggle that was seen to be ahead! On 12 April Portal received warning of this from Air Ministry; the Air Staff considered that the anticipated attack on France and the Low Countries would be decisive, and warned that Bomber Command must not wear its strength away over Norway. Five days later Pierse, the Vice Chief of Air Staff, instructed Portal that, although for the present the Command's main effort should be against Norway, it should be prepared to switch the effort to Germany with the least possible delay should the situation develop. Portal had something of a problem: he was being ordered to attack, yet at the same time to conserve his strength. He was undoubtedly much relieved when the evacuation of central Norway lessened the calls on Bomber Command.

A week later, having in the meantime received a

reminder from the Secretary of State for Air that he was still expected to conserve the Command's strength, Portal was told by Pierse to carry out intensive attacks against the airfield at Vaernes near Trondheim. This target was at the very extreme of Bomber Command's range. The intention of these attacks was to curtail enemy air action over and around Narvik until local fighter cover could be provided there.

Portal reacted strongly. Writing to Pierse on 5 May, he voiced his objections to this order in no uncertain terms: '...in my opinion a decision to institute these operations, even on the minimum scale likely to have any appreciable effect, would not be compatible with the directions from the Secretary of State which I received yesterday about the conservation of our bomber strength'. He pointed out that only the Hampden squadrons would be suitable for this task, and that he considered these squadrons should not be subjected to further attrition. Portal pointed out that the Hampden was the only aircraft his Command possessed suitable for minelaying operations. 'I do not know,' he continued, 'how much importance the Air Staff attach to these operations as compared with bombing, but in my own view they are likely to be the most effective employment of our force in the war next to the bombing of industrial targets. It seems to be the height of folly to throw away the experienced "gardening" crews on the bombing of aerodromes which, I think you will agree, shows the least result for the loss of equipment expended'.

On 10 May this argument was settled when Germany invaded France and the Low Countries; Portal and his staff at HQ Bomber Command in their despatch on the Norwegian campaign, however, made the point clearly that from 13 April the Command had been operating under close direction from Whitehall. 'The control of the operation of my Command,' it reads, 'was virtually assumed by the Air Ministry. Although my advice was often sought, I was not responsible for the selection of objectives nor for deciding the effort to be employed'. Strong words indeed; the experience probably decided him later, when he was Chief of Air Staff, to allow greater scope to the commander of his bomber force.

Bomber Command's operations during the Norwegian campaign were improvised in response to a totally unexpected attack by the enemy. Plans for the use of the Command in the event of an enemy attack on France and the Low Countries had, however, been long prepared. The decision had to been taken that the Blenheim squadrons of No.2 Group, together with two Whitley night bomber squadrons of No.4 Group, should collaborate in delaying the German advance. The squadrons were to remain in Britain, but their detailed tasks were to be arranged by the staff at HQ British Air Forces in France; this headquarters could not directly order operations by Bomber Command, only request them. Bomber Command was not obliged to meet these requests if they were considered impracticable. This 'collaboration' plan was known as Plan WA (Western Air) 4b.

Though committed to assist the land forces, Bomber Command aircraft were not intended for use on battlefield targets. Their role was to bomb communication points, bridges, major cross-roads, etc, behind the German advance. This was not a task for which the Blenheims were really suitable, their low speed and pathetic defensive armament made them sitting targets for enemy fighters. The RAF possessed no fighter/bomber aircraft in 1940, and so the least unsuitable aircraft, the Battles of the Advanced Air Striking Force and the Blenheims of Bomber Command, were used to attack enemy communications. The advancing German armies and their lines of communication were well protected by anti-aircraft guns and fighters. Within a few days the Advanced Air Striking Force was taking terrible losses, the Battles being lost at the rate of one in every two despatched. On 14 May forty out of seventy-one Battles were lost attempting to break the German bridgehead at Sedan. The same evening seven out of twenty-eight Blenheims were lost in a further attempt to hold up the German advance at this point. At 4·50 am on 17 May twelve Blenheims of 82 Squadron took off from their base in England to attack an armoured column at Gemblous in Belgium. At 8·20 am a single Blenheim returned to 82's base at Watton. The other eleven had been lost in the attempt to halt the German column. There is no doubt that the Blenheim squadrons would have been wiped out had not Portal insisted that they operate only with a fighter escort. This enabled Bomber Command to carry out daylight attacks over Northern France and Belgium as the enemy drove toward the Channel ports; as the Germans closed in on Dunkirk the Command's Blenheims were still playing their part in the evacuation of the armies; harrying the encircling Germans.

When the rescued troops returned to Britain there were several instances of RAF personnel being physically assaulted by Dunkirk veterans and the cry was raised, 'Where was the RAF?' This was understandable; troops being fiercely attacked by enemy aircraft during a headlong retreat were unable to understand why they could not see any British aircraft overhead to protect them. Bomber Command's aircraft were there, attacking the advancing enemy columns and taking grievous losses in doing so. There is ample evidence in German records that good work was done by both the Command Blenheims and the Advanced Air Striking Force Battles. RAF fighters also played a valiant part in the battle. Little recognition has been accorded the RAF pilots and aircrews who fought the air battles over France and the Low Countries in a desperate effort to aid their comrades on the ground. Whilst the Blenheims were trying their hardest to harry and delay the advancing German armies, what of the Command's 'strategic' bombers, the 'main force' of Wellingtons, Whitleys and Hampdens?

On 10 May, as Winston Churchill took office as Prime Minister, there was immediate pressure that the RAF's strategic bombers should attack Germany itself. That same night thirty-six bombers were sent to attack München-Gladbach, on the west bank of the Rhine and a key communication centre behind the German armies.

Permission to attack targets east of the Rhine was still withheld and bombing of Germany was confined to attacks on communications west of the Rhine. But, on 14 May, the last restraints in the bombing war gave way when the Germans bombed Rotterdam. This attack was widely reported and gave rise to a feeling of revulsion throughout the world. It should be explained, at this point, that this raid was not a 'terror' attack as was widely reported at the time.

The German units attacking Rotterdam were held up by strong Dutch resistance. The Germans issued an ultimatum: if the Dutch did not surrender, bombers would be used to attack the Dutch positions in the city. As the ultimatum expired 100 Heinkel 111s took off en route for Rotterdam. During their flight to their target the Dutch units in Rotterdam surrendered and a recall order was sent to the Heinkels. Forty-three returned to base without bombing but fifty-seven had dropped their bombs before receiving the recall signal. 250-kilogram bombs were used and these were dropped fairly accurately but the bombing started fires with which the Dutch fire brigade were unable to cope. The resulting blaze, completely out of control, caused severe damage in the city and killed over one thousand Dutch civilians. The Germans could, therefore, be said to be correct in their claim that this was not a 'terror' raid on an unprotected city, but a tactical attack on enemy positions in support of their ground troops that went terribly wrong. It must be said, however, that the raid was in support of a completely unprovoked invasion of a neutral country, a country that had been neutral even during the First World War. Whatever one's views on the bombing of Rotterdam, it was this attack that put an end to the restrictions on the bombing of targets in Germany.

On 15 May Prime Minister Churchill and his War Cabinet finally gave permission for Bomber Command to attack targets east of the Rhine and on that night ninety-nine Whitleys, Wellingtons and Hampdens attacked oil plants, marshalling yards and other targets in the Ruhr.

The operations of Bomber Command during 1939 and early 1940 have been described in some detail to illustrate that, whatever occurred later, the British Government held back its bomber force for over eight months after war commenced and even for four days after the Germans invaded France and the Low Countries. Britain had tried to avoid the bombing of built-up areas in which German civilians might have been casualties in the vain hope that the German government too would restrain their bombers.

By 10 May 1940, when the so-called phoney war abruptly ended, Bomber Command had flown 990 night sorties for the loss of twenty-eight aircraft and 393 daylight sorties with a loss of forty-five aircraft. It had already been calculated that the Command could not sustain a loss rate of more than 5 per cent on continuous operations and hope to survive. The loss rate on the daylight operations had been 11·5 per cent while that for the night flights had been 2·8 per cent. Because of these loss rates Bomber Command was to become primarily a night bomber force.

The Strategic Bomber Offensive could be said to have started on the night of 15 May 1940, and from that date the theory that strategic bombing of industrial centres rather than the tactical bombing of ships and military targets would decisively influence the course of the war was to be put to the test. The Strategic Bomber Offensive was to last for almost exactly five years. For Bomber Command it was to be a long hard road: there would be disappointment, agony and grief but there would also be awesome success and triumph. The story of the bomber crews would be one of tears and laughter, of tragic losses and magnificent raw courage. The Command entered upon the campaign in May 1940 as a weak under-strength force; it would stand at the end of the offensive in May 1945 as the most powerful striking force in all British history. Its five year campaign would also end in doubt and bitter controversy.

CHAPTER FOUR

S hortly after he had taken up his command at High Wycombe, Sir Charles Portal had been involved with planning for the possibility of a German invasion of Britain. On 7 May an inter-Service conference had been held at the Air Ministry to discuss the employment of the air forces in the event of invasion. Portal learned, to his surprise, that there was no accepted view of the Germans' most probable course of action. There was no agreement on what part of the coast the enemy assault was likely to fall. Would the Germans try to seize a port, or land on open beaches? What types of assault vessels would they employ? To these and other questions Portal required answers in order that Bomber Command could make effective plans against an enemy assault. Bomber Command finally got some idea of the answers in May, just as the German breakthrough into Northern France created a dangerous and difficult situation.

Despite the apparent confusion at higher levels, and the pressure of calls on the Command during the catastrophe of May and June, the staff at High Wycombe made good progress with the Command's anti-invasion plans. Although the bombers would retain some of their wider responsibilities and operate as necessary against industrial sources of supply in Germany, the main task would be to strike against German shipping. The principal targets would be the landing craft in the Channel ports and, in the event of successful enemy landings, the Command's aircraft would be required to attack enemy troops.

In the event of invasion the Command's training organisation would also be used, aircraft and crews from the Operational Training Units would be thrown into the battle, and instructors from Training Command would be required to use their obsolete Hart and Audax biplanes for dive-bombing. During June the Group Commanders were ordered by High Wycombe to improve the defences on their airfields. At the end of June the operational airfields were in a well-prepared condition for any attacks upon them by paratroops or other enemy units. It certainly could not be said of any Bomber Command airfield, as Air Vice-Marshal Harris remarked of a Training Command field near one of his No.5 Group units, that it was 'defended by one Local Defence Volunteer with rheumatism and a shotgun'.

During the following weeks a stream of directives reached High Wycombe from the Air Ministry. Portal was first directed to make the reduction of the German air effort against Britain his first priority. Accordingly he sent his aircraft mainly against targets connected with the German aircraft industry and enemy airfields in France and the Low Countries. Then he was ordered to switch the main effort onto German ports and shipping. On 13 July another Air Ministry directive ordered the Command to concentrate once again on the reduction of the German air effort, and listed fifteen primary targets. This time Portal reacted strongly. His sharp reply included a point by point criticism of the directive; this criticism pointed some of the ways in which the future bomber offensive would develop. Of the fifteen primary targets, Portal commented, only three could be expected to be found by average crews on moonlit nights. He also pointed out that most of these targets were too far east to give the crews time for any extended search. He complained that the Air Staff's elimination of targets south of latitude 51 degrees north would have the effect of grounding his force when the weather was bad in the north. His final point was that practically all the primary targets listed were isolated: bombs which missed them would achieve no other useful purpose. All these arguments were to be reiterated later by Harris, when he was Commander in Chief, but in stronger terms!

Portal's criticisms were basically tactical, but he did not hesitate to criticise the strategy itself. Writing to Sir Sholto

Douglas, who was then the Deputy Chief of Air Staff, on 17 July he said, 'in Bomber Command we have the one direct offensive weapon in our whole armoury, the one means by which we can undermine the morale of a large part of the enemy people, shake their faith in the Nazi regime and, at the same time and with the very bombs, dislocate the major part of their heavy industry, much of their chemical industry and a good part of their oil production'.

The Air Ministry did not accept all of Portal's arguments, but he was given an extended list of targets in a further directive dated 24 July. Bomber Command was, however, to find support in the person of Prime Minister Churchill. On 20 July Churchill asked Portal what could be done about bombing Berlin. Portal explained the possible weight of attack against the city, and told the Prime Minister that his Command had plans ready for the strategic bomber force to be used at twelve hours' notice, at any time after 1 August.

Thus it happened that when the first German bombs fell on central London on 24 August, Bomber Command was ready to retaliate, and did so instantly by sending eighty bombers to attack Berlin the following night. Other raids on Berlin were mounted in the same week. Although only minor material damage was done to the city, there is little doubt that these attacks, together with earlier attacks on industrial targets in Germany, had a chastening effect on the Germans, who had been promised by Goering that, 'No enemy bombs would fall on the Third Reich'. Hitler was stung into ordering the Luftwaffe to concentrate its attack upon London, instead of the RAF's fighter airfields, and this proved to be the turning point in the Battle of Britain.

This service to the Battle of Britain by Bomber Command was, of course, indirect. Of direct help to the battle – the bombing of the invasion barges in the Channel ports – as the Commander in Chief had anticipated, had far more effect than any bombing of enemy airfields. During the first week of September the concentration of barges became such as to positively invite attack, and on the night of 7 September the Wellingtons, Whitleys and Hampdens began to add their bombloads to those of the Blenheims.

Night after night the crews attacked 'Blackpool Front' as they called the invasion coastline stretching west from Dunkirk. The targets were near at hand, maximum bombloads could be carried and results were impressive. Barges were set ablaze in Calais docks, Boulogne, Dunkirk and many other points along the coast. In two weeks of intense maximum effort Bomber Command crippled, according to German records, at least twelve per cent of the German invasion fleet.

RAF Fighter Command, of course, won the Battle of Britain in the savage air fighting over south-east England, and the people of Britain will never be able to repay the debt this country owes to the magnificent young pilots who fought those battles. It should not be forgotten, however, that Bomber Command also played its part in the Battle of Britain. It was Bomber Command's attacks on the German invasion fleet which caused the German High Command to disperse the fleet well before Hitler's decision of 12 October to abandon the invasion.

Little credit has ever been given to Bomber Command for the part it played in preventing the German invasion of Britain, although the American historian Telford Taylor in his book *The Breaking Wave: the German defeat in the summer of 1940* sums up the Command's contribution: 'these raids contributed to the decision for ultimate postponement, and it is beyond question that they caused the dispersal of enemy shipping which began on 20 September, and which made reinstitution of the invasion alert a lengthier process and a far more unlikely process than before'.

With the threat of invasion removed, the Command turned its attention once again to the industrial targets in Germany. Night after night the Whitleys, Wellingtons and Hampdens flew out into the blackness, over the flakships stationed off the Dutch coast where the crews knew the Luftwaffe had now begun to fly standing patrols of night fighters, and on over the darkness of Germany. To the crews who flew during the main bomber onslaught of 1943–1945, bomber operations of that autumn of 1940 would have seemed rather amateurish affairs. Each aircraft captain chose his own route, often his own time of take-off. It was left to individual pilots to decide the height they would fly, and the height at which they would attack. The overwhelming majority of crews who operated during the autumn of 1940 and through 1941 were conscientious airmen who did their best to find and hit their assigned targets but they were operating under tremendous difficulties. The aircraft were fitted with inadequate ancillary equipment; the only navigational aid the navigator was supplied with was a sextant. The aircraft were without heating and the cold was appalling, the crews flew clothed in layers of silk, wool and leather and yet they were still bitterly cold. Vital systems jammed, wings iced up for lack of adequate de-icing gear, guns froze and the crews' limbs seized with the cold.

The navigator gave his pilot a course on take-off, and then relied upon dead reckoning navigation, hoping to be able to establish pinpoints on the ground below at intervals in the six or seven hour flight. If the night was clear and the stars could be seen, then it was possible for the navigator to obtain a position fix with his sextant providing the pilot was willing to fly straight and level for long enough. It was sometimes possible for the wireless operator to obtain a loop bearing from England, but there were instances where an error in obtaining the bearing could put the aircraft on a 180 degree reciprocal course; the Germans also jammed the wavelengths. Navigators, therefore, tended to treat wireless bearings with a certain amount of suspicion. Before take-off navigators were given a weather forecast which included predicted winds. Often the predictions were inaccurate and the winds were blowing the aircraft off track. The crews could attempt to check drift by dropping a flare; this was at best a chancy business and quite impossible in low cloud.

In those early days of the bomber offensive, it was usual to send the aircraft out on moonlit nights in an effort to assist navigation and help in finding the target. Often, however, cloud blanketed the ground even on moonlit nights. If trying to bomb a target blanketed by cloud, crews had only two alternatives: to descend recklessly low through the cloud to attempt to identify the target or to bomb on ETA (Estimated Time of Arrival) at the target. Bombing on ETA could create errors of tens, scores and sometimes even hundreds of miles. Many of the crews in the early days of 1940–1941 lost their lives because, rather than drop their bombs on ETA, they descended to impossibly low heights attempting visually to identify their target, and fell victim to enemy anti-aircraft fire. There were, of course, some crews who were unwilling to descend through the cloud and bombed on ETA. Bomber Command issued memoranda to all Groups concerning the practice of bombing on ETA, and it must be made clear that the vast majority of crews genuinely attempted to identify their targets before bombing. Again and again during this period the enemy were unaware that Bomber Command had been attempting to attack a specific target. Bombs were being dropped all over Germany, on villages, farms, and homes, as well as on factories and industrial regions.

At the same time that British bombers were desperately struggling to find and bomb specific targets in Germany, the Luftwaffe bomber force was attacking Britain. The Luftwaffe had the advantage of Knickebein, a form of radio direction beam. Using this navigation aid, which was far in advance of anything Bomber Command would possess for some considerable time, the enemy attacked cities the length and breadth of Britain such as London, Birmingham, Liverpool, Plymouth etc.

Portal suggested on 1 September that twenty German towns be 'proscribed', warned by radio that they would be attacked one by one, following each occasion on which a British town was bombed by the Luftwaffe. It was while Portal was Commander in Chief that a memorandum was circulated in Bomber Command reminding all pilots that 'in industrial areas there are invariably a very large number of targets. In view of the indiscriminate nature of the German attacks, and in order to reduce the number of bombs brought back ... every effort should be made to bomb these'. Some historians have inferred that by this instruction Portal was, in effect, encouraging his crews to drop bombs indiscriminately on Germany. The truth is that Portal was a realist, after each night's operation the staff at HQ Bomber Command studied the debriefing reports of the crews who had groped through the night sky over Germany desperately searching for their assigned target, an oil plant or factory, which Portal suspected they seldom reached. Portal took the attitude that it was preferable to bomb any target in an industrial area rather than have his crews risk their lives needlessly.

There were some senior officers at Air Ministry who were shocked at Portal's attitude, and on 5 September Sir Richard Pierse wrote to the Prime Minister that there was 'little doubt that the reason for the effectiveness of our night bombing is that it is planned and relentless until the particular target is knocked out or dislocated, whereas German night bombing is sporadic and mainly harassing'. In the Air Ministry's directive on 21 September the priorities for Bomber Command were once again spelled out: 'precision' attacks on invasion barges, the aircraft industry and oil plants were to continue. The only concession to Portal was the final paragraph authorising occasional morale attacks on Berlin 'although there are no objectives in the Berlin area of importance to our major plans'.

In the Official History *The Strategic Air Offensive against Germany*, Sir Charles Webster and Dr Noble Frankland say that, in strategic bombing, civilians would be bound to be killed, and that hospitals, churches and cultural monuments would also be hit. They say that the Air Staff, as represented by Sir Richard Pierse, accepted this only in so far as it was inevitable; the Official Historians then go on to say, 'Bomber Command, as represented by its Commander in Chief, Sir Charles Portal, now believed that this by-product should become an end product in itself. He believed the time had come to launch a direct attack on the German people themselves'. This claim is grossly unfair to both Bomber Command and its commander. There are many survivors of Bomber Command's war who disagree profoundly with much in the Official History for reasons which will be dealt with later.

To Pierse and some others around him at the Air Ministry at that time, it seemed that Portal was recommending indiscriminate bombing, and this minority opposed him for this reason. To the majority of those around him, particularly his staff at High Wycombe, Portal seemed absolutely correct. They were aware that, after months of attempting night 'precision' bombing, the targets the bomber crews had attempted, with great courage, to find and attack, were barely touched. One thing is certain: the populations of Britain's cities who were experiencing the effect of German area bombing would have wholeheartedly supported Portal's attitude.

Sir Cyril Newall, Chief of Air Staff, retired on 4 October 1940 and was replaced by Sir Charles Portal. Sir Richard Pierse, probably the foremost advocate of 'precision' bombing, took over as Commander in Chief of Bomber Command. It is worth making the point here, especially in view of the comment in the Official History accusing Portal of wishing to launch a direct attack on the German people, that as Chief of Air Staff he could have immediately ordered an area bombing campaign. In this he would have had the full support of the Prime Minister; Churchill was urging such a proposal throughout the winter of 1940 and the spring of 1941. Churchill wrote to the Air Ministry on 2 November

'We have seen what inconvenience the attack on the British civilian population has caused us, and there is no reason why the enemy should be freed from all such embarrassments'.

Portal gave no such order. For the next year he allowed Pierse to continue on the course the new commander favoured, attempting precision attacks on chosen industrial targets. It was only when this policy was seen to have signally failed that it would finally be abandoned. This surely gives the lie to Webster and Frankland's comment and also to those historians who have used this comment in the Official History to accuse this fine commander of wishing to institute 'terror' bombing.

Proof that Portal's concern with attacking the German morale was only a secondary consideration and that his main concern was that Bomber Command's crews should not 'waste' their bombs and their lives needlessly, is contained in his directive to Pierse of 30 October 1940 ordering him to attack Berlin and other German cities:

'As many heavy bombers as possible should be detailed for the attack, carrying high explosive, incendiary and delay action bombs with perhaps an occasional mine... The objectives considered most suitable for these concentrated attacks are the sources of power, such as electricity generating stations and gas plants, and centres of communication; but where primary targets such as the oil and aircraft industry objectives are suitably placed in the centres of the towns or populated districts, they also might be selected.'

It is clear from this directive that Portal's attitude was that, whilst Bomber Command should continue to attempt to attack precise targets, if the targets were situated in the centre of populated areas then any bombs that went astray would hit workers' homes, etc, and thereby, hopefully, have some effect on the workers' morale. This could hardly be called a deliberate policy of indiscriminate or 'terror' bombing.

In December 1940 the Lloyd Committee on German oil resources made their report, claiming that Bomber Command had achieved a 15 per cent reduction in enemy fuel production. The report said that this had been achieved by only 539 tons of bombs; 6·7 per cent of the total Command effort since the summer. This was a quite remarkable claim, since the Germans were hardly aware that their oil resources had been the target for a systematic assault. It is a measure of the complete inadequacy of British economic Intelligence that the Lloyd Committee could reach these quite amazing conclusions. Little wonder that later in the war Harris professed little faith in experts at the Ministry of Economic Warfare. This report became the basis for continuing attacks on oil throughout the spring of 1941.

All through the latter part of the winter of 1940–1941 and well into the spring, Pierse's crews continued to struggle over Germany in vain attempts to hit the oil plants, but with little success. A few bombing cameras were now becoming available; these were given to the more experienced crews in the squadrons. When these crews released their bombs a photoflash was also released and the automatic camera photographed the crew's bombing position. The first careful analysis of these target photographs revealed that few crews were obtaining aiming-point photographs. Despite this evidence Pierse pressed ahead with his policy of 'precision' night bombing. It was the escalation of the Battle of the Atlantic which diverted Bomber Command from its offensive over Germany.

In the face of the mounting U-boat threat, and the threat posed by German capital ships, the Air Ministry issued a directive to Bomber Command on 9 March 1941, ordering the Command to concentrate on the U-boat bases at St. Nazaire, Bordeaux and Lorient together with the *Scharnhorst* and *Gneisenau* at Brest. All through that summer of 1941 the bomber crews dropped their bombloads onto these targets, again with little result. This was no fault of the crews who pressed home their attacks in the face of intense opposition. The truth was that the bombs the crews were dropping were incapable of penetrating the thick concrete U-boat pens and not powerful enough to do a great deal of damage to the two battle cruisers.

As 1941 slipped away the Prime Minister was becoming increasingly disturbed by the shortcomings in the results that Bomber Command had achieved. He was also aware of the difference in the thinking of Portal and Pierse regarding bombing policy; it was doubtful, however, if even Churchill understood the full extent of the failure of bombing policy thus far. Lest anyone reading this should think that, in speaking of failure, any criticism is intended of the crews, it should be made quite clear that this is not so. The failure was not that of the crews; the failure was the commander's. Sir Richard Pierse had little grasp of operational realities and an almost arrogant belief in the correctness of his 'precision' bombing policy. His crews, for their part, had very little confidence or faith in their commander and many of the more experienced crews felt they were achieving little despite the sacrifice of most of their comrades.

The aircrews of Bomber Command displayed great courage during 1941 for very little practical result. On the night of 7 July a Wellington of No.75 Squadron was taking part in an attack on Münster, a town in the industrial Ruhr valley, when it was attacked by a night fighter on its homeward journey. The second pilot was a young New Zealander, Sergeant James Ward. Ward later broadcast an account on the BBC, anonymously, of the events that night and the verbatim transcript, although understated in typical RAF manner of the time, is a story of selfless courage and heroism:

'It was on one of those Münster raids that it happened. It had been one of those trips that you dream about – hardly any opposition over the target; just a few searchlights but very little flak – and that night at Münster I saw more fires than I have ever seen before. We dropped our bombs right in the target area and then made a circuit of the town to see what was going on before the pilot set course for home.

'As second pilot I was in the astrodome keeping a look out all round. All of a sudden, over the middle of the Zuider Zee, I saw an enemy machine coming in from port. I called up the pilot to tell him, but our intercom had gone phut. A few seconds later, before anything could be done about it, there was a slamming alongside us and chunks of red-hot shrapnel were shooting about all over the place. As soon as we were attacked, the Squadron Leader who was flying the plane put the nose down to try and dive clear. At that time we didn't know that the rear-gunner had got the attacking plane, a Messerschmitt 110, because the intercom was still out of action and we couldn't talk to the rear-gunner.

'We'd been pretty badly damaged in the attack. The starboard engine had been hit and the hydraulic system had been put out of action with the result that the undercarriage fell half down, which meant, of course, that it would be useless for landing unless we could get it right down and locked. The bomb doors fell open, the wireless sets were not working and the front gunner was wounded in the foot. Worst of all, fire was burning up through the upper surface of the starboard wing, where a petrol feed-pipe had been split open. We all thought we'd have to bale out, so we put on our parachutes. Some of us got going with the fire extinguisher, bursting a hole in the side of the fuselage so that we could get at the wing, but the fire was too far out for that to be any good. Then we tried throwing coffee from our flasks at it, but that didn't work either. It might have damped the fabric round the fire, but it didn't put the fire out.

'By this time we had reached the Dutch coast and were flying along parallel with it, waiting to see how the fire was going to develop.

'The Squadron Leader said, "What does it look like to you?" I told him the fire didn't seem to be gaining at all and that it seemed quite steady. He said, "I think we'd prefer a night in the dinghy in the North Sea to ending up in a German prison camp." With that he turned out seawards and headed for England.

'I had a good look at the fire and I thought there was a sporting chance of reaching it by getting out through the astrodome, then down the side of the fuselage and out onto the wing. There was a rope there; just the normal length of rope attached to the rubber dinghy to stop it drifting away from the aircraft when it's released on the water. We tied that round my chest, and I climbed through the astrodome. I still had my parachute on. I wanted to take it off because I thought it would get in the way, but they wouldn't let me. I sat on the edge of the astrodome for a bit with my legs still inside, working out how I was going to do it. Then I reached out with one foot and kicked a hole in the fabric so that I could get my foot into the framework of the plane, and then I punched another hole through the fabric to get a hand-hold, after which I made further holes and went down the side of the fuselage onto the wing. Joe the navigator was holding onto the rope so that I wouldn't sort of drop straight off.

'I went out three or four feet along the wing. The fire was burning up through the wing rather like a big gas jet, and it was blowing back just past my shoulder. I had only one hand to work with getting out, because I was holding on with the other to the cockpit cover. I never realised before how bulky a cockpit cover was. The wind kept catching it and several times nearly blew it away and me with it. I kept bunching it under my arm. Then out it would blow again. All the time, of course, I was lying as flat as I could on the wing, but I couldn't get right down close because of the parachute in front of me on my chest. The wind kept lifting me off the wing. Once it slapped me back onto the fuselage again, but I managed to hang on. The slipstream from the engine made things worse. It was like being in a terrific gale, only much worse than any gale I've ever known in my life.

'I can't explain it, but there was no sort of real sensation of danger out there at all. It was just a matter of doing one thing after another and that's about all there was to it.

'I tried stuffing the cockpit cover down through the hole

in the wing onto the pipe where the fire was starting from, but as soon as I took my hand away the terrific draught blew it out again and finally it blew away altogether. The rear-gunner told me afterwards that he saw it go sailing past his turret. I just couldn't hold onto it any longer.

'After that there was nothing to do but to get back again. I worked my way back along the wing and managed to haul myself up onto the top of the fuselage and got to sitting on the edge of the astrodome again. Joe kept the dinghy rope taut all the time and that helped. By the time I got back I was absolutely done in. I got partly back into the astrohatch, but I just couldn't get my right foot inside. I just sort of sat there looking at it until Joe reached out and pulled it in for me. After that, when I got inside, I just fell straight onto the bunk and stayed there for a time.

'Just when we were within reach of the English coast the fire on the wing suddenly blazed up again. What had happened was that some petrol which had formed a pool inside the lower surface of the wing had caught fire. I remember thinking to myself, "This is pretty hard after having got as far as this." However, after this final flare-up the fire died right down – much to our relief, I can tell you.

'The trouble now was to get down. We pumped the wheels down with the emergency gear and the pilot decided that, instead of going to our own base, he'd try to land at another aerodrome near by which had a far greater landing space. As we circled before landing he called up control and said, "We've been badly shot up. I hope we shan't mess up your flarepath too badly when we land." He put the aircraft down beautifully, but we ended up by running into a barbed wire entanglement. Fortunately nobody was hurt though, and that was the end of the trip.'

For his act of supreme heroism, in climbing out onto the wing of the Wellington in an attempt to extinguish the blazing wing, Sergeant Ward was awarded the Victoria Cross. Tragically, he was to go 'missing' on a later operation.

By August 1941 Bomber Command had been operating for fifteen months in the strategic role of bombing German industrial targets. Although the small force available to the Command could not be expected to deliver a decisive blow against the enemy, the question of whether the bombing was having any real effect was now being raised. Lord Cherwell, the Prime Minister's personal scientific adviser, had requested Mr D. M. Butt of the Cabinet Secretariat to carry out an independent survey on the current performance by the Command against targets in Germany and France. The Butt report was presented in August 1941. Lord Cherwell had been doubtful for some time of the results being achieved by bombing and the report confirmed, in fact exceeded, his worst fears.

On any given night around one-third of the crews returned without claiming to have attacked the primary target. Mr Butt, therefore, analysed only the target photographs of the remaining crews who had claimed to have bombed their primary targets during the months of June and July. He reported that only one-third of these crews had actually come within five miles of the target. Against targets in the Ruhr the proportion fell to one-tenth. Mr Butt also made the point that on moonlit nights two crews in five came within five miles of their target; on moonless nights this figure fell to one in fifteen.

Sir Richard Pierse was not inclined to accept the findings of the report, claiming it was incompatible with the amount of damage he considered had been done to targets in Germany.

The Butt report, however, came as a major shock to one man: the Prime Minister. On 3 September he sent a personal note to Chief of Air Staff Portal together with a copy of the report. The note reads: 'This is a very serious paper, and seems to require your most urgent attention. I await your proposals for action'.

The Butt report was the low-water mark in the fortunes

of Bomber Command. Since the outbreak of war the Command's aircrews had attempted, with great determination, to attack precise targets, such as warships, oil plants, factories, electricity generating stations, gas plants and military airfields. In almost all these attempts they had failed. This was no fault of the crews: they had first been sent against naval targets in daylight, flying ill-armed aircraft in unescorted formations which were hacked down by the Luftwaffe fighters. Later, they had been required to attempt to find and bomb precise targets in Germany at night using the barest minimum of navigational aids. Despite all their difficulties the crews had achieved some success; the *Scharnhorst* and *Gneisenau* had been damaged, 100,000 tons of shipping had been sunk by mines dropped by 'gardening' crews. A wide variety of industrial plants had been slightly damaged and the Focke-Wulf aircraft factory in Bremen, together with a number of other plants, had begun to disperse their operations: more in anticipation of future damage than any present attacks. One courageous pilot had won the Victoria Cross in an attack which closed the Dortmund-Ems canal for ten days in 1940. A few thousand Germans had been killed, and immense labour was being diverted to the construction of air-raid shelters. Anti-aircraft guns and searchlights were being greatly strengthened. A few oil plants had been temporarily shut down because of slight damage. All this, however, had done no really significant damage to the German war economy.

The report caused great debate in political and service departments. Politicians such as Sir Stafford Cripps, Lord Privy Seal and Leader of the House of Commons, were opposed to bombing in principle and lost no opportunity of making their views known to the Prime Minister. In reality, although Cripps made his own feelings clear, he had no real influence on Churchill, who was unmoved by his arguments for diverting the bomber force to other theatres of war, e.g. the Middle and Far East. Churchill had witnessed the

German area bombing of British cities and was determined to repay the enemy in kind: there were few people in Britain at that time who would not have wholeheartedly supported the Prime Minister's attitude.

Churchill was not intent on stopping the bomber offensive against Germany, he was concerned with its apparent failure so far and was intent on making it more effective. The Prime Minister pressed the claims of the bomber offensive with all his remorseless energy: a proposed force of 4,000 heavy bombers was discussed. It would, in fact, have been impossible to produce a front-line strength of 4,000 heavy bombers from Britain's industrial resources, but it is an indication of the Prime Minister's determination to proceed with the bomber offensive that on 7 September, only days after the Butt report landed on his desk, he should write:

'In order to achieve a first-line strength of 4,000 heavy and medium bombers, the RAF require 22,000 to be made between July 1941 and July 1943, of which 5,500 may be expected to reach us from American production. The latest forecasts show that, of the remaining 16,500, only 11,000 will be got from our own factories. If we are going to win the war, we cannot accept this position.'

Since Churchill knew perfectly well that production forecasts invariably failed to be met, this note should not be taken too literally, or be regarded as evidence of his commitment to a 4,000 bomber plan. It was another of Churchill's famous notes, to drive the production departments to greater effort.

Churchill was determined that the bomber offensive should proceed and increase in intensity, he knew that in Bomber Command he had the only force with which Britain was capable of taking the war to Germany. But in what way was Bomber Command now to proceed; what was the Command to seek to achieve? Since the late summer of 1940 the Air Staff had realised that unescorted daylight bomber operations against Germany were out of the question. Since the RAF had no long-range fighters to provide any escort, daylight operations were not feasible. Some airmen had hopes of their eventual long-term resumption and these hopes would be fulfilled brilliantly in the later stages of the war, but for the foreseeable future there was no question of operating in daylight over Germany. There might be very occasional precision attacks at night, when and if the opportunity arose, and when a vital target required special attention. The Butt report had, however, proved conclusively that, at this stage of the war, the majority of Bomber Command's crews were unable to find and hit a precise target at night. A new bombing policy had become inevitable.

CHAPTER FIVE

During the autumn of 1941 the Butt report was given urgent consideration at Air Ministry and by the War Cabinet. The decision was finally made at the end of 1941 that, since with the equipment then available to the crews it appeared that a city or large industrial area was the best that they could be expected to hit under average conditions, Bomber Command would abandon the effort to hit precise targets and direct its attacks against the urban areas of Germany. Although brilliantly successful precision attacks would be mounted later in the war, three-quarters of the total tonnage of bombs dropped by the Command were dropped on area targets. Area bombing was, therefore, the major part of Bomber Command's war.

Churchill had no moral scruples about attacking German cities; after all the Luftwaffe had carried out area attacks on British cities. A prime example was Coventry; in November 1940 the Luftwaffe had devastated Coventry, 400 bombers attacked the city in wave after wave, totally destroying 20,000 houses, killing 600 people and injuring 1,000 more. Some historians have accused Bomber Command of initiating area bombing in the Second World War; they ignore the fact that the RAF had attempted to attack precise targets, albeit unsuccessfully, for fifteen months whilst the Luftwaffe was laying waste Britain's cities. Another point that should be noted is that, even during the height of the coming onslaught on Germany, Bomber Command never descended, at any time, to pure terrorism. The cities attacked were always of industrial, military, or communications importance.

Certain writers have argued that, by embarking on a systematic attack on cities, the British sacrificed their own moral case and contributed to the terrible moral collapse that took place later in the war, especially in the treatment of prisoners and civilians in the concentration camps. This is pure cant. Britain was fighting a war of survival against one of the most evil regimes the world has ever known. She was faced with catastrophe on almost every front, her cities had been mercilessly area-bombed by the enemy, her leaders were conscious of the terrible suffering that Nazi Germany was inflicting upon the rest of Europe. The choice for the directors of Britain's war effort was a clear one – area bombing of Germany or no bombing offensive at all. It is easy for liberal writers, looking back on this issue from the comfort of their armchairs forty years later, to condemn the decision taken in 1941. Most of these critics were either not born or were young children in 1941, and have no real conception of the stark reality of the situation facing Britain at that time. One thing is certain; if the government of the day had asked the people of Britain to vote on the question of area bombing there would have been very few negative votes.

Churchill, at any rate, had no doubts. He was aware that Bomber Command was the only weapon he had capable of striking at the heart of Nazi Germany and so the decision to switch the main weight of the attack onto the urban areas was taken. Between the delivery of the Butt report and the beginning of the concentrated attack on the German cities, however, there was a pause.

In the autumn of 1941 Bomber Command's casualties had begun to rise at an alarming rate. In the first eighteen nights of August, 107 aircraft were lost. In September, 76 aircraft failed to return and a further 62 crashed in England. In October, 68 were missing and 40 crashed. On the night of 7 November 37 aircraft failed to return from 400 despatched. Including those aircraft which crashed in England, the entire front-line strength of the Command had been statistically lost in less than four months. During 1941, a bomber had been lost for every ten tons of bombs dropped; admittedly the Command would suffer higher losses in 1943, but by then the entire context of the war had changed. At the end of 1941 this loss rate was unacceptable, particularly when the Butt report made it clear that no significant results were being achieved for the loss of these aircraft and crews. There was, by now, little confidence in Sir Richard Pierse's direction of the Command. His crews had little faith in the man at the top; to the crews he appeared to have little grasp of operational realities. Pierse had also lost the confidence of those in authority above him. On 13 November he was instructed by Air Ministry to reduce the number of sorties against Germany, especially in bad weather. The War Cabinet, said the directive, 'have stressed the necessity for conserving our resources in order to build up a strong force to be available by the spring of next year'.

In fact the strength of Bomber Command gained little from this pause; there was a constant drain of squadrons being despatched to Coastal Command to aid in the Battle of the Atlantic, and other squadrons were sent to bolster Britain's sagging fortunes in the Middle and Far East.

In these months, however, the Command was beginning to re-equip with new aircraft. The Whitleys and Blenheims were being phased out and the new generation of heavy four-engined bombers was beginning to arrive. The twin-engined Avro Manchester was a disappointment, the Rolls Royce Vulture engines which powered this aircraft were unsatisfactory, and the crews of No.5 Group who had to fly this aircraft considered themselves distinctly unlucky. Avro's brilliant designer Roy Chadwick was, however, already working on this problem, and by increasing the wingspan and replacing the two Vulture engines by four Rolls Royce Merlins, the unsatisfactory Manchester was to be metamorphosed into the Lancaster, the finest bomber of the Second World War. Also, the new four-engined Short Stirling and the early Handley Page Halifax, which would look inadequate in 1943/4, were in 1941/2 a vast improvement on the aircraft they were replacing.

The spring of 1942 promised not only better aircraft, but

also the means to navigate with greater accuracy over Europe. The scientists had come up with a radio-pulse system, code named GEE, with which a navigator could fix his position by signals from three transmitting stations in Britain. It was believed that when GEE was issued in quantity to Bomber Command, early in 1942, it would take the Germans at least six months to devise a method of jamming it. By the autumn of 1942 it was hoped to introduce still more advanced equipment. The scientists at Telecommunications Research Establishment at Malvern were working on a range of equipment that would, by the end of the war, make Bomber Command the most technically complex force the Allies possessed.

Bomber Command had a new policy, it was beginnings to receive new equipment; the Air Staff decided it needed a new commander. Sir Richard Pierse was relieved of his command; there was little sympathy in Bomber Command. He had inspired little confidence among his crews and little affection among his subordinate staff at High Wycombe; he had forfeited faith in his judgement in high places. He paid the price for being the man in command at the lowest ebb in Bomber Command's fortunes. It was decided to find a new commander, untarnished by the failures of the past.

One evening in December 1941, during the Washington conference between the American and British war leaders, Portal took Harris to one side. Harris, who had earlier been in charge of No.5 Group, had been promoted to Air Marshal and was now head of the RAF delegation in the United States. Portal offered Harris the post of Commander in Chief, Bomber Command; Harris immediately accepted. He would be in command for the rest of the war.

Arthur Travers Harris was born at Cheltenham on 13 April 1892, the son of George Steel Travers Harris and Caroline Maria Harris, and educated at Gore Court and Allhallows School, Devon. In 1910 he went to Rhodesia to try his hand at gold mining and later drove a mail coach, then became a tobacco planter. At the outbreak of the First World War in 1914, he enlisted in the 1st Rhodesia Regiment, with which he served as a private in South West Africa. When the unit was disbanded in 1915, Harris left for England and learnt to fly at Brooklands. In November 1915 he obtained his pilot's licence and joined the Royal Flying Corps as a Second Lieutenant. He saw action in France as a fighter pilot before returning to Britain in early 1918 as commander of a home defence unit. He was one of the pioneers of night flying and fighting and was awarded the Air Force Cross in November 1918.

After the war he was granted a permanent commission in the newly formed Royal Air Force with the rank of Squadron Leader. In 1921 he commanded No.31 Squadron in India before taking command at No.45 (Troop Carrier) Squadron in Iraq. Whilst serving in the Middle East as a Squadron Commander he pioneered the prone position for bomb aiming; his two flight commanders at this time were Flight Lieutenants Robert Saundby and the Hon. Ralph Cochrane. The three men would serve together again when Harris took up his appointment at Bomber Command: Saundby as his Deputy Commander, and Cochrane as Air Officer Commanding No.5 Group.

From 1933 to 1937 Harris served in staff posts at Air Ministry, in 1937 he commanded No.4 Group. He went to America in 1938 to head the RAF Purchasing Mission. At the outbreak of war on 3 September 1939, Harris was in command of No.5 Group; in his time there he established a reputation as a forceful commander of bomber operations. In 1940 he was Deputy Chief of Air Staff under Portal; he was at Air Ministry for only six months before going to America as head of the RAF Delegation in Washington.

Many adjectives are applicable to Harris; he was dedicated, single-minded and ruthless. A man of boundless energy and explosive temperament, he was supremely confident of his own judgement and did not suffer fools gladly. He was not a cunning or devious man; he was blunt, sometimes to the point of rudeness, but he was, above all things, straightforward and honest.

From the beginning of the war Harris had been convinced that, given the shortcomings of Britain's armed forces compared with those of Germany, a strategic bombing offensive was inevitable. This was the man who would rule Bomber Command from its Headquarters at High Wycombe for more than three years and have a profound influence on the course of the war.

CHAPTER SIX

S ir Arthur Harris took command of Bomber Command
on 22 February 1942, just seven weeks before his
50th birthday. Awaiting Harris on his desk was the Air
Ministry directive issued to Bomber Command on 14
February 1942: this directive was the blueprint for the future
onslaught on German cities and centres of industrial
production, and removed the previous constraints on
targeting. The winter order to conserve the Command's
strength was withdrawn. The directive instructed the new
commander, 'You are accordingly authorised to employ your
forces without; restriction'. Under the heading 'Primary
Industrial Areas' were Essen, Duisburg, Dusseldorf and
Cologne. 'Alternative Industrial Areas' included Lübeck,
Rostock, Kiel, Hanover, Bremen, Mannheim, Frankfurt,
Schweinfurt and Stuttgart. The directive ordered, 'continuing
attacks on Berlin ... to maintain the fear of attack over the
city and to impose ARP measures'. It was stressed that
during the expected six months' life of GEE, the Command
must concentrate the weight and density of its attack as never
before. Essen was suggested for the earliest attacks, the
remainder of the cities on the list would follow. Lest there be
any confusion in the mind of the new commander about
objectives, Chief of Air Staff Portal wrote on 15 February;
'Ref. the new bombing directive: I suppose it is clear that the
aiming points are to be the built up areas, not, for instance,
the dockyards or aircraft factories ... This must be made
quite clear if it is not already understood'.

In recent years a number of writers have appeared to
labour under the delusion that the area bombing policy was
entirely Harris's creation: they have either not understood, or
have preferred to ignore, the fact that the policy had been
decided before Harris took up his command. Undoubtedly

Harris wholeheartedly supported the policy: he was an early convert to the concept of strategic bombing, and had been an advocate of the 4,000 bomber idea which it was apparent would never be fulfilled. Area bombing, however, was not his creation, although he applied himself to executing the policy laid down for him by those in authority above him with energy, dedication and single-mindedness.

Harris took command at a time when the Allies' fortunes were at their lowest ebb: the Japanese had destroyed the American Pacific Fleet at Pearl Harbour; Hong Kong and Singapore had surrendered, the *Repulse* and *Prince of Wales* had been sunk; Rommel was triumphant over the British Army in Libya. Harris was convinced that Bomber Command was the only means by which Britain's strategy would move from the defensive – which he was certain spelt ultimate defeat – to the offensive, which offered a prospect of eventual victory. The Command had been given a new policy and a new leader; Harris knew, however, that its survival depended upon its performance in the immediate future. Harris had taken over Bomber Command at the nadir of its fortunes: it was under threat of extinction, not from the enemy, but from the Admiralty, the Army and those politicians who had no faith in a strategic bomber offensive. He had inherited a front-line strength of less than 400 bombers, almost 100 fewer than were available three months earlier when the order had been given to conserve the Command's strength over the winter months. This was due to two reasons: the Whitleys, Hampdens and Blenheims were being phased out and replaced by newer types, and the Command had been forced to loan some of its squadrons to Coastal Command for use by the Admiralty in the Battle of the Atlantic. Many aircraft and crews had also been sent to the Middle East at the insistence of the War Office.

Harris was well aware that he had to score some successes quickly, but the force at his disposal was lamentably small. It was with a normally available force of only 300 operationally serviceable aircraft, of which only 50 were heavy bombers, that Harris began his long campaign against the industrial cities of Germany. He bitterly resented the drain of his aircraft to Coastal Command and the Middle East, but it was something he was unable to stop immediately and the loss of his crews and aircraft continued for some time. He was determined to infuse a new confidence in the Command; and it is a measure of this remarkable man's force of personality that, within only a few days of his taking over as Commander in Chief, somehow everyone in the Command was convinced that this was the turning point. Almost immediately the legend of Harris was born in Bomber Command. This apparently remote man, who was in fact close to every activity and need of his men, who had developed bombing techniques which were the basis of modern methods in the 1920s, and who had helped lay the foundation of Bomber Command, had arrived at High Wycombe to lead and direct the force in which he so passionately believed. From the day he arrived no officer on his staff had any doubt about the future of the Command: the fear of an assassination of Bomber Command by the admirals, generals and doubting politicians receded. Bomber Command began to hold its head high.

One of the first proposals to reach Sir Arthur Harris at High Wycombe in February 1942 came from the Foreign Office. They wanted to revive Portal's old idea of proscription: to name publicly, by radio, twenty German towns and cities that would be subjected to saturation attack by Bomber Command: hoping for panic among the population, a mass exodus of refugees and a rising tide of terror. Harris would have nothing to do with this suggestion. He was aware that the Command, as yet, possessed inadequate strength for the sort of wholesale destruction that the Foreign Office wanted; and he certainly had no intention of allowing the enemy to concentrate defences around preordained targets.

Harris intended to commence his campaign by attacking across the widest possible front; in doing so, he hoped to divert enemy resources from the offensive to the defence of his own cities. But as Bomber Command fought to prevent its extinction by its critics, foremost of which was the Admiralty which wanted the Command's aircraft for use in the Battle of the Atlantic, he knew he had to obtain some quick, spectacular successes to silence the critics. In his early months in command he produced a succession of operations which, in comparison with what had gone before, were brilliantly successful.

On 9 March he despatched 235 aircraft to attack the Renault factory at Billancourt, which produced 14,000 trucks a year for the Wehrmacht. The Command attacked in a new pattern, led by a first wave of flare-dropping aircraft, followed by a wave of bombers carrying maximum loads of incendiaries to attempt to set fire to the target, followed by the main force carrying high explosive bombs. This attack was an early step on the road to evolving a target-marking pattern. Approximately 470 tons of bombs were dropped on Billancourt. When the bombing photographs were analysed it was apparent the attack had been a great success. The concentration of bombs on the Renault plant was exceptional; the plant was later reported to have lost two months' production.

Since taking command on 22 February, Harris had despatched his aircraft to attack Essen and other targets in the Ruhr as ordered by the February directive from the Air Ministry. He had, however, not been satisfied with the results: targets in the Ruhr were extremely difficult to attack successfully due to the industrial haze in which the area was perpetually covered. On the list of targets in the Air Ministry directive was the town of Lübeck, a Baltic port, the centre of which was of medieval construction. Although Lübeck was beyond GEE range the device was of great value on the flight to the target, and the town's position at the mouth of a river made final identification comparatively easy for the crews. On 28 March Harris despatched 191 bombers to attack the town. Ten Wellingtons dropped flares over the target; they were followed by a wave of forty aircraft carrying only incendiaries. The following waves of bombers were loaded with incendiaries and the new 4,000 pound high capacity bombs; these new heavy bombs would become the main weapon of the new generation of heavy bombers.

The attack was carried out at very low level, many aircraft attacking from as low as 2,000 feet. Over 200 acres of Lübeck were destroyed, four factories, the electricity generating plant and the main railway station were severely damaged. 1,425 houses were totally destroyed and 1,976 badly damaged, 312 people were killed. In London the Ministry of Economic Warfare estimated it would take at least seven weeks for Lübeck to resume full industrial production.

This attack was the first real success in the Command's new policy of area bombing; it was a personal victory for the leadership of Sir Arthur Harris. With this attack, compressed into 140 minutes, Harris had begun the concentration of effort that would dominate the future bombing offensive, the Command seeking to bomb within the shortest possible time, saturating the German defences and fire-fighting services. Timing over the target was of vital importance, routeing was to develop into an art. The days of crews making their own individual attacks, 'by guess and by God,' as they used to describe them, were coming to an end. At this stage it was difficult to assess the full potential of GEE. The crews equipped with the new device were, of course, taking a little time to become fully proficient in its use. The navigator operated the set from a receiver mounted above his navigation table; by timing the pulses received from three transmitting stations in England, whose signals appeared as lines on a small cathode ray tube, he could 'fix' the aircraft's position on charts marked with special GEE grids. Accuracy depended on each navigator's proficiency, but it had become clear during the attacks on the Ruhr targets that GEE was not sufficiently precise to be used as a blind bombing system. GEE was, however, an excellent aid to navigation – the first one the crews had been provided with – and it gave them great confidence.

After some further unsuccessful attacks on targets in the Ruhr, and some of the less dangerously defended German cities, Harris committed the Command to the second of his devastating area attacks. This time the target was the North German coastal town of Rostock, another lightly-defended old city. The attack commenced on the 23 April and continued over four nights.

Rostock was a seven hour round trip and was well beyond the limit of GEE range. The attacking force was divided, part being ordered to attack the city itself, the remainder the Heinkel aircraft factory just beyond the southern suburbs. The first two attacks, on 23 and 24 April, were disappointing; the third and fourth raids, by 128 and 107 aircraft respectively, were considered successes to match that of Lübeck. By the third night the Germans had gathered every gun they could from northern Germany to defend Rostock, and the anti-aircraft fire was fierce; despite this the crews pressed home their attacks at low level. When the bombing photographs were analysed the crews were told by HQ Bomber Command that they had carried out one of the most successful attacks of the war. Thousands of people fled in panic from the ruins and the surrounding villages and towns became temporary refugee camps. Goebbels declared hysterically, 'Community life in Rostock is almost at an end'.

In the Official History Webster and Frankland wrote, 'Thus, by the end of April 1942, Bomber Command, under the vigorous leadership of Air Marshal Harris, had shown, not only to Britain's Allies, but also to her enemies, the tremendous potential power of the long-range heavy bomber force'.

The attacks on Lübeck and Rostock were blazoned

across the headlines of the popular press and were a much needed boost for the morale of the British people. Harris himself did not regard the targets as vital ones, although Lübeck was an important port for the supply of German armies in North Russia and Scandinavia, as well as for the import of strategic materials from Sweden, a major supplier to Germany. Rostock contained industries of importance and military installations. The real importance of these attacks to Bomber Command was to learn to what extent a first wave of aircraft could guide a much larger second wave to the target by starting a large conflagration. Harris was developing his ideas on the principle of the best crews leading the way and marking the target. This was not a new idea to Harris: in his days in the Middle East as a squadron commander he had experimented in illuminating targets with flares, but found that existing flares were not satisfactory for this purpose. He had continually pressed for the development of satisfactory marker bombs and flares for use by target-marking crews.

Harris insisted on being well briefed on the experiments on new devices for greater accuracy in navigation and bombing, and pressed hard for greater priority to be given to their development; constantly raising the matter with Portal, the Chief of Air Staff. But although he was aware of these experiments, he was also well aware that they would not help him to improve the effectiveness of his bombing offensive for some considerable time; therefore he concentrated on building up the strength and size of his force.

Despite the success of Lübeck and Rostock, there was still considerable opposition to the concept of a strategic bombing offensive, particularly from the Admiralty. Harris knew that to silence this opposition he needed to mount a brilliantly successful attack, that would be so dramatic in its results that not only would it quell the opposition, but would capture the weight of British public support for Bomber Command.

The Commander in Chief also wanted to prove for himself that his crews could achieve industrial destruction on a decisive scale against a major target. Lübeck and Rostock had proved that a small lightly-defended town could be seriously damaged by a concentrated attack of two or three hundred bombers, but what would be required to achieve the same effect on a major city, or a large seaport such as Hamburg? Toward the end of April 1942 Sir Arthur Harris conceived a brilliant, imaginative idea: a force of one thousand aircraft would attack a major German city in one night – this would be the greatest concentration of air power the world had yet seen. There was, of course, no military significance in the figure of one thousand aircraft, but Harris well knew that the effect of a successful operation with one thousand bombers would be immense.

At the beginning of May Harris did have approximately one thousand aircraft under his command; but this included the aircraft and crews of the Operational Training Units and Heavy Conversion Units. These crews were not fully trained, although some had slight experience of dropping leaflets over France. To use these aircraft and crews on the operation Harris planned presented many dangers. He had available a front-line strength of some 400 bombers, most of them now equipped with GEE, but to throw in the OTU and HCU aircraft, meant he would not only be committing his entire front-line strength, but also all his reserves, in a single operation. If the force were to suffer heavy losses, which it could well do, the Command's whole programme of expansion and training could be seriously jeopardised.

Against this, however, were the great advantages to be gained if the attack were successful. There would be the tremendous effect on the British public as well as the Americans and Russians. The result of using a powerful force against a major target would be plain for all to see; Harris considered that only such a demonstration of the potential power of Bomber Command would prevent demands from the Royal Navy for more of his bombers to be transferred to Coastal Command. He also considered it would enable him to obtain more aircraft, crews, radar and navigational aids, which the Command so desperately needed.

After carefully considering all the advantages and disadvantages of the plan, he took his idea to Portal. Harris told Portal that an attack of such strength and magnitude would, if successful, surely bring powerful support from both official sources and public opinion. He continued that it would prove, beyond doubt, that Germany could be effectively attacked by bombing, and that it would force the Germans to divert much military resource to the defence of the homeland against attack from the air. Portal, however, required very little persuasion: he was as great a believer in the bomber offensive as Harris, and gave the plan his blessing at once. Portal told Harris they would require powerful political support to overcome the opposition that would inevitably come from the Admiralty.

Harris went to see Prime Minister Churchill and told him the whole plan. Churchill listened to Harris intently; and gave him his full backing. Harris told the Prime Minister the Command expected the losses to be less than five per cent, i.e. 50 aircraft; Churchill told Harris he would be prepared to accept a loss of 100 aircraft on an operation of such magnitude.

For such a colossal attack it was obvious that a full moon and good weather would be essential; the next full moon period was 26 May to 30 May. If Harris was to put this audacious plan into operation soon, then the choices were limited. The next moon period would be late June: then July. With his great daring and boldness Harris decided on May.

But even before the 'Thousand Plan' was finally approved, Bomber Command was to receive even more demands for the transfer of aircraft and crews to Coastal Command and the Middle East; this at a time when the Command's planning staff were making forward preparations for the great attack. On 11 May an outraged Harris wrote to Portal:

'With your knowledge of the crew position in my Command, and of the constant drains which are inflicted on my OTU outputs and my operational units, you may agree that there is justification for a rising sense of anger, if not despair, at the way the other Commands (and indeed some departments of the Air Ministry) regard Bomber Command as a milch cow whenever they feel the slightest pangs of hunger or even mere inconvenience within their own organisations.

'This robbery has gone on for so long, and is so persistent and rhythmic in its recurrence, that I was wondering whether you would now issue an instruction to other Commands and departments concerned that they are once and for all to disabuse themselves of the idea that Bomber Command is their natural and proper source of revenue whenever they feel that they would like to increase their own forces. I wonder what sort of outcry would arise if Bomber Command demanded and expected as a matter of course fully trained crews from Coastal and Army Co-operation Commands every time it expanded'.

On 13 May Portal wrote to tell Harris that Coastal and Army Co-operation Commands had been instructed that they could no longer call on Bomber Command for trained crews and must, in future, provide from their own resources.

Harris visited Portal at Air Ministry on 18 May and gave him further details of the plan, informing Portal that Bomber Command was looking for 250 to 300 aircraft from other Commands, mainly Coastal Command, to make up the figure of 1,000. Portal contacted the First Sea Lord, and informed Harris by letter that it appeared there would be no objection to participation by Coastal Command. Letters were sent from HQ Bomber Command to Coastal, Fighter, Training and Army Co-operation Commands giving details of the plan and asking for the maximum possible contribution. In this letter Harris expressed his intention in his usual blunt, straightforward way, '...to annihilate one of Germany's main industrial centres by fire'.

Sir Philip Joubert, the Commander in Chief Coastal Command, promised 250 aircraft, and was full of enthusiasm for the plan. Harris and the Deputy Commander Sir Robert Saundby were still suspicious of the Admiralty, and this suspicion was indeed well founded. The attack was planned for the night of 27/28 May, or the first night within the moon period which provided suitable weather conditions. On 25 May the Admiralty ordered Sir Philip Joubert that, under no circumstances, was Coastal Command to play any part in the attack. On hearing of this it is understood that Harris commented, 'Typical Admiralty bloody-mindedness'!

With the figure of aircraft available standing at approximately 800, Harris refused to give up, and called for a last-minute effort from the Command to raise the required further 200 aircraft and crews from within Bomber Command itself; the weather was kind to him, for it was not until the night of 30/31 May that it was sufficiently good for the attack to go ahead. In the groups and squadrons the ground staff put in magnificent work to make the required extra aircraft available and, by obtaining many 'scratch' aircrews from group and station staff, the figure of aircraft available rose to 1,046, of which only four were from Training Command. The Admiralty's refusal to allow Coastal Command to take part had the opposite effect to that intended: the Thousand Plan would go ahead and it would now be entirely a Bomber Command effort. The choice for the target was to be between Hamburg and Cologne; the decision for the attack to proceed was taken by the Commander on the morning of 30 May, and weather dictated that the target would be Cologne.

The force attacked in three waves led by the Wellingtons of No.3 Group; Air Vice-Marshal Baldwin, Air Officer Commanding No.3 Group, flew in one of his group's aircraft. Behind the Wellingtons came the rest of the huge force. Crews in the last wave flew over Germany, unable to believe the reality of the vast red glow ahead of them; some crews thought the Germans had lit a huge dummy fire to deceive them. As they drew nearer the target they realised the awesome truth: the glow was the city of Cologne ablaze from end to end. A pilot of 50 Squadron flying that night was Flight Lieutenant H. B. Martin. Martin, who was to become a legendary figure in Bomber Command, was already an experienced pilot but that night as he flew over Cologne at a height of 4,000 feet he and his crew were awed by the spectacle beneath them. Like so many crews that night, they had never seen anything like it before.

Between 00·47 and 02·25 that morning, 3,330 houses were destroyed, over 2,000 badly damaged, more than 7,000 partly damaged. 12,000 fires raged in the city, the water-mains were breached, gas-mains exploded, power cables were severed and the telephone system wrecked. 36 factories were completely destroyed, 70 severely damaged and more than 200 others damaged. The docks and railway system were badly damaged and the tram system dislocated for months.

85 soldiers and civil defence workers were killed, together with 384 civilians; almost 5,000 people needed first aid treatment. 45,000 people were made homeless. The full extent of the damage to the city could not be assessed by Bomber Command for several days because of the black pall of smoke which rose to over 15,000 feet above the city. For Cologne the attack was a catastrophe.

Goering, Head of the Luftwaffe, refused to believe the first reports to be received from Cologne, claiming that it was impossible for Bomber Command to have mounted an attack of such weight. But as later reports were received, Goering learned the truth; Cologne was in a state of utter chaos.

The attack made huge headlines on both sides of the Atlantic. *The Times* reported, 'OVER 1,000 BOMBERS RAID COLOGNE'; 'Biggest Air Attack of The War' read headlines in other papers. Congratulations poured in to Bomber Command Headquarters from all quarters. Churchill said, 'This proof of the growing power of the

British Bomber Force is also the herald of what Germany will receive city by city from now on'.

The Command had lost forty aircraft in the raid, 3·8 per cent of those despatched; well below the estimated 5 per cent, and nowhere near Churchill's 'acceptable' figure of 100. A quiet young man named Leslie Manser was the pilot of a 50 Squadron Manchester flying from 50's base at Swinderby against Cologne: his bomber was badly hit over the target, and he faced a long struggle to get it home to England. It became obvious that the Manchester could no longer remain airborne, and Manser ordered his crew to bale out, waving away the parachute his flight engineer offered him as he struggled to keep the aircraft steady long enough for his crew to jump. His crew got out of the aircraft but the pilot was unable to get clear himself. Leslie Manser was posthumously awarded the Victoria Cross for his selfless heroism in sacrificing his life in an attempt to save his comrades.

Bomber Command carried out two more '1,000 Plan' attacks before the huge force had to be dispersed to avoid disruption of the Command's training programme. Neither of these attacks was a significant success. The targets were Essen and Bremen and only a slight amount of damage was done to either city.

The Command now settled to spend the rest of the summer of 1942 attacking Germany on a wide front, with far less weight and intensity, and with results that could not compare with the devastation wreaked on Cologne. Harris could now afford to bide his time; in only four months as Commander in Chief he had revitalised the whole Command, established his own reputation, delighted the Prime Minister who greatly admired Harris's daring and boldness; and made an immense contribution to the British people's morale at a time when the nation's fortunes were at their lowest ebb. The British people, and the politicians, were awed by the scale and power of the '1,000 Plan' attacks, but they were only a pinprick compared to the devastation Bomber Command would wreak in 1943 and 1944. Harris himself said, 'We are going to scourge the Third Reich from end to end'. After the area bombing of Britain's cities, the terrible scars of which were only too visible, the people of Britain obtained great satisfaction and comfort from Harris's words and the deeds of his Command. Unlike some of his masters Harris was not a devious man; his was an honest, blunt character. No hypocrite, he made no attempt to conceal the true nature of area bombing, and gave clear notice of his intentions: unfortunately, the same cannot be said of his political masters who were most circumspect in attempting to conceal the true nature of area bombing of enemy cities.

Some writers have described Harris's '1,000 Plan' attack as a gigantic confidence trick, claiming it achieved no real result and only succeeded in diverting to Bomber Command resources which could have been more usefully employed elsewhere. Most of these writers base their criticism of Harris on their own aversion to the concept of a Strategic Bomber Offensive, and in doing so fail to understand Harris's motives (or perhaps prefer to ignore them) in carrying out the attack on Cologne. Harris's motives were: to prove beyond all doubt the potential power of Bomber Command, to prove that Germany could be effectively attacked by a powerful bomber force, to put an end to the draining away of his strength by demands from other Commands, to obtain backing for his Command from both public and politicians, to boost British morale and to force the enemy to divert more military strength from other fronts for the defence of his homeland against air attack. To do this he took the bold gamble of risking his entire front-line strength, together with his entire reserve, in one audacious attack. He succeeded brilliantly in all his objectives; and in doing so proved himself to be a great military commander.

CHAPTER SEVEN

During 1942 the twin-engined medium bombers were phased out of service and replaced by the new generation of heavy four-engined aircraft, although some of the Wellingtons remained in service until 1943. The disappointing Manchester was also replaced by the Lancaster, much to the relief of the 5 Group crews who had been unfortunate enough to have to operate the Manchester.

The Avro Lancaster was undoubtedly the great heavy bomber of the Second World War. It was without vices and easy to fly; a gentleman's aircraft according to its pilots. It cruised at 216 mph, with a top speed of 266 mph, at an official ceiling of 22,000 feet, although on many occasions its crews flew well above its official maximum height. With a bombload capacity of 14,000 lbs it had a range of 1,660 miles. This bombload was more than the load carried by two American B 17 Flying Fortress aircraft: later in the war the Lancaster was modified to carry the 22,000 lb. Grand Slam Bombs.

The other two new aircraft were disappointing; the Stirling was unable to operate much above 14,000 feet and was the first target for German anti-aircraft gunners and night-fighter pilots: the early Halifaxes had alarming vices in the air and some Halifax crews were more frightened of their aircraft than of the enemy! After many modifications, the Halifax Mark Three came into service in early 1944; this was a superb aircraft and the crews who flew the Mark Three rated them equal to, if not better than, the Lancaster.

The new heavy bombers carried a crew of seven: pilot, navigator, bomb-aimer, flight engineer, wireless operator and two air-gunners. The second pilot had been dispensed with and, depending on the aircraft type, either the flight engineer or bomb-aimer acted as pilot's mate on take-off and landing, sitting in the second pilot's seat and assisting the pilot with the throttles.

The crews had been fully trained in their own specialist duties before joining Bomber Command. The pilot, navigator and bomb-aimer had joined the RAF in the PNB group. These men had usually gone overseas for training; to South Africa, Southern Rhodesia or Canada under the Empire Air Training Scheme, or to America under an agreement made before America entered the war. The flight engineer, wireless operator and gunners had all been trained in the United Kingdom.

The crews would form up at the Operational Training Units, where they would commence training as a crew on Wellingtons or Whitleys. Sufficient personnel for the OTU intake, usually sixteen crews, would be assembled in one of the hangars and told to form themselves into crews: at this stage only the rear-gunners would be there, the mid-upper gunner and flight engineer would join the crew later. In the first few days at OTU a rather bewildered milling herd of aircrew formed themselves into crews by a process of natural selection. One distinguished bomber pilot has described this as 'like a lot of little dogs sniffing at each other'.

This process may seem strange to anyone who has no knowledge or experience of Bomber Command, but it was actually quite logical. The senior officers in the Command understood very well that the fate of the aircrews, indeed the very future of the Command, depended on the integrity of the men, and the mutual confidence and faith that crew members had in their colleagues. It was decided, therefore, that there would be no arbitrary assembling of men into operational aircrews, and every opportunity was given to allow like-minded men to crew up together.

'I believe you want a navigator. Can you land a Whitley without breaking it?'

'I was talking to a gunner this morning, he seems to know his stuff. I thought he might do for our crew; I've asked him to have a beer at lunch-time. See what you think of him.'

In this seemingly casual manner men banded themselves together as crews, to face what would be the supreme test of their lives.

All these young men had probably originally wanted to be pilots, in fact, the navigators and bomb-aimers had volunteered under the PNB scheme, hoping to qualify as pilots, but had been remustered during training. Those who survived the rigorous selection and training to qualify as pilots could be considered the elite. There were often half-serious complaints from other aircrew that it was a pilot's air force. To some extent this was true, but it should be remembered that the pilot was responsible in the air for the crew's lives, and it could be by his decision that the other crew-members lived or died. In the event of trouble the pilot had to remain at the controls until the crew had escaped, and every pilot was aware that, when the moment of final decision came, he stood the least chance of escape. The action of Leslie Manser, in sacrificing his own life to give his crew a chance to escape over Cologne, was an example of the selfless courage every pilot knew would be required of him if the moment came.

A bomber crew was a mutually dependent team, and each man in the crew made a vital contribution to its survival, and to its success on operations. The navigator's responsibility was to keep the aircraft on track at all times, to ensure that the aircraft adhered to the meticulous timing of the operational flight, to reach the target at the allotted time, to avoid defended areas and, at the end of the operation, to find the home base safely. The navigator could never relax on an operational flight and had to work out complicated mathematical problems. Most navigators were well-educated, sensitive men; there was a large proportion of former or future schoolmasters among them. They were inclined to be a little clannish and had a sort of unofficial 'navigators union'. Generally navigators were inclined to be quiet, reserved types; considered probably the least warlike of aircrew members. There were, however, some notable exceptions to this general rule.

The bomb-aimer was introduced into the crews during 1942: until that time the navigator had been responsible for aiming and releasing the bombs. When the aircraft was on its bombing run up to and over the target the bomb-aimer, lying in the prone position pioneered by Harris over twenty years earlier in Iraq, was in control of the aircraft and the pilot obeyed his instructions until the bombload was released and the bombing photograph taken. The bomb-aimer assisted the navigator by attempting to map read, when weather conditions made this possible, from his position in the nose. Later in the war, as new devices became available to the crews, the bomb-aimer would carry additional responsibilities. The bomb-aimer was often the pilot's mate and became the reserve pilot in case of emergency; like most navigators they were often men who had failed to complete a pilot course.

The pilot; navigator and bomb-aimer, the PNB group, were considered by those in authority to be the brains in the crew; as far as the crews were concerned, however, there was no distinction. There was great comradeship between all crew members, far more comradeship than existed in any other branch of the three services. Few crews even realised that the PNB group officially existed.

The wireless operator sat near the navigator and was responsible for all contact with the base. As operations were conducted in wireless silence, as far as the aircraft were concerned, he rarely had much to do except listen for the half-hourly broadcasts from base. These contained the coded broadcast winds, very occasionally a recall signal, but rarely anything else. For this reason most pilots employed the wireless operator as the crew odd-job man, using him to deal with any minor emergency that arose in any part of the aircraft. If the aircraft got into serious difficulty, however, then the wireless operator was vital. His radio fixes could establish the aircraft's position, and if ditching became inevitable he remained at his post until the last possible moment sending the aircraft's distress signal.

The flight engineer, who joined the crew when they had completed the OTU course, had also been introduced in 1942. He took a great deal of routine work away from the pilot, monitoring the instruments, working out fuel consumption, etc. In some aircraft he acted as pilot's mate, instead of the bomb-aimer, and assisted the pilot with take-off and landing. In emergency he too was vital, because his fuel calculations had to be accurate. Over enemy territory he was often used as an extra look-out man; some engineers were also the reserve bomb-aimer.

All the above crew members worked together in the front part of the aircraft where there was some degree of heating for them and each man had a certain freedom of movement. The two air-gunners were completely isolated in their turrets. Dressed in cumbersome layers of heavy clothing, forced to remain in their cramped turrets for many hours, they had the loneliest and most uncomfortable job in the crew. They were, however, vital; for on their alertness and vigilance depended the survival of the whole crew. They were trained to an extremely high standard of marksmanship; their main responsibility, however, was to instruct the pilot on evasive action by anticipating attacks from night fighters. In the event of combat with a fighter, it was the gunners who were effectively in control of the aircraft and a good operational pilot obeyed their instructions instantly. Many gunners survived their tour of operations without firing their guns in anger; the best gunners, in fact, were those who knew when to hold their fire and not draw attention to their aircraft's presence. The average operational flight for a gunner consisted of sitting for seven or more hours in extremes of cold, vigilantly searching the darkness of the night sky, hoping against hope that he would see a German fighter in time to take evasive action before the fighter opened fire.

As a matter of interest, it is worth mentioning at this point that the scientist Freeman Dyson, who later went to the Princeton Institute for Advanced Studies, was in 1944 working in the Operational Research Section of Bomber Command. Dyson argued that gun turrets should be removed from the heavy bombers, thereby increasing their speed, Dyson appears to have deeply impressed himself with this argument. He claimed that his research showed that experienced crews had no better chance of surviving a tour of operations than novices and that it was a matter of chance which aircraft were shot down. He made this the basis of an indictment of Bomber Command, published in 1979 in the *New Yorker* magazine, claiming that the RAF showed no interest in his research. As an ex-operational Bomber Command aircrew member I am not surprised at Bomber Command's attitude. On two occasions my life and the lives of my crew were saved by the alertness and vigilance of my rear-gunner Flight Lieutenant Philip Bailey. I am certain that any experienced crew member would agree with me that two good, vigilant gunners were worth far more than the extra speed that Dyson's suggestion would have given. All experienced aircrew were well aware that, no matter how experienced or good a crew, luck still played a great part in survival. Dyson only reveals his total lack of grasp of operational realities in making this claim; it was not Bomber Command's leaders who were out of touch; it was Freeman Dyson.

Having formed themselves into crews the rather bewildered novices would spend some weeks at their Operational Training Unit learning tactical and technical skills that a year ago crews had been compelled to learn over Germany. The accident rate at the OTUs was high, on some courses it reached twenty-five per cent. Tour-expired aircrew posted to instruct at OTUs soon learned that teaching novice crews operational skills in tired and worn out aircraft was not exactly a rest cure.

At the end of their training these eager young men were posted to their operational groups. Little huddles of humanity clad in air force blue could be found waiting on obscure small railway stations to be collected by a nonchalant WAAF

MT driver. Those destined for 3 Group could be seen in East Anglia, for Nos.1 and 5 Groups it was Lincolnshire and 4 Group crews Yorkshire. In these counties well over half of these young men would make their final homes.

The mood of Bomber Command at the end of 1942 and through 1943 was very different from that of 1939. The majority of the squadrons were no longer stationed on the pre-war airfields with the comfortable brick-built quarters. During 1942 the eastern part of England was being transformed into one gigantic aircraft carrier; hastily built wartime airfields now carpeted the countryside. The squadron personnel were learning to live with Nissen huts and wooden buildings surrounded by chronic mud. The concrete runways and dispersed hardstandings with their four-engined bombers were the important part of the new fields; the rest, the living quarters, the mess halls, the technical sites, etc, were hastily erected temporary buildings. It was to one of these wartime airfields that most aircrews found themselves transported. Those lucky enough to end up at a pre-war 'gin-palace' considered themselves highly privileged.

The aircrew, as befitted men who were statistically not long for this world, were provided with whatever comforts and privileges the wartime RAF could give them. The service provided luxuries unheard of in wartime, such as extra milk, sugar, fruit juice and real eggs. There was sunray lamp treatment in the medical quarters; they were dosed with halibut oil capsules and only had to undertake the most essential duties when not flying. The crews were entitled to the privilege of 6 days' leave every 6 weeks; if the weather was good aircrews might operate at least 8 or 9 times a month. Some crews never lived to see their first leave pass. A good squadron commander could create a good squadron spirit, but to many crews the squadron, or even the flight, meant little. One kept close company with one's own crew and perhaps one or two others who arrived at the same time.

Crews drank, womanised, sometimes even went on leave together, regardless of individual rank. Rank meant nothing to the crews; many were captained by a Sergeant pilot who could, in the air, be in command of commissioned officers among his crew. In the White Hart in Boston, or Betty's Bar in York, non-aircrew personnel were surprised to see, for example, a Squadron Leader pilot and a Sergeant air-gunner drinking pints of beer together, and addressing each other by their first names. The crews were too close to death to bother with formalities of rank; through 1942 the loss rate in the Command, including crashes in England, seldom fell below 5 per cent – one aircraft in every twenty on every operation. A crew was required to complete a minimum of thirty operations to complete their tour. One did not need to be a mathematical genius to work out the chances of survival! In the air these seemingly sloppy, ill-disciplined men, were among the most highly-disciplined fighting men Britain has ever produced; they had to be, to stand any chance of survival. There were, at times, dark mutterings about the ill discipline and the general behaviour of the crews; mainly from desk-bound administrative types. These self-important people, who seemed at times to consider they were doing more for the war effort than the crews, had rarely flown, even as passengers, and they had no conception of the tight discipline of a good operational aircrew in the place where it mattered; in the air over enemy territory.

By contrast, the aircrews enjoyed excellent relations with the ground crews, the men and women who serviced and maintained their aircraft. Between the air and ground crews there developed a mutual respect and affection. There was also a respect between the staffs of the operations sections, flying control, signals section and the crews. Many of these sections were staffed largely by WAAF personnel; some of these girls became closely acquainted with the crews and were badly hurt emotionally when a crew they were particularly fond of went missing. Some of the local people from the villages around the airfields appeared to regard these girls as some kind of scarlet women; little did they know there was surprisingly little immorality on the bomber stations.

Many aircrew preferred to relax in each other's company with a drink rather than women. For those who did crave female company, it was difficult for a WAAF to refuse a boy who could be dead within a few days. One attractive WAAF, at an airfield in Yorkshire, offered her favours to a nineteen-year old youngster, who still blushes to recall that he turned her down – because, although he had a distinguished record on operations, he was afraid of her! Meeting the lady again, nearly 40 years later at a Squadron reunion, he at least had the grace to apologise for his churlish behaviour.

It was, in fact, remarkable that in the frenzied parties that celebrated a 'stand-down ', the award of a decoration or the end of a crew's tour of operations, so many of these youngsters retained their innocence.

By the end of 1942 the strange routine of a bomber station had become a way of life. The crews rose late, and went to their respective messes for breakfast. By 11 am they were waiting around the flight offices to hear whether operations were 'on' that night. Some days they were 'stood down'; they then made a dash for the nearest town. Opportunities for a day 'in town' were limited and the crews made the most of them. Often they were told operations were on, and would begin all the day's preparations only for the operation to be cancelled later in the day, usually around 4 or 5 pm. Many crews hated these 'scrubs', as they were called; they had to go through all the nerve-racking preparations for operations; fighting a battle against fear and anticipation all day. Others took a more philosophical view, quoting an oft repeated adage, 'Never curse a scrub. It could have been the "op" you were due to go missing on'. More often than not, it was the prospect of bad weather over the bases in the early hours that caused the cancellation. There had been some bad nights in the past when poor weather had caused crashes all over the eastern counties of England.

If 'ops' were on, the armourers began the task of preparing the bombloads. In the late morning the aircrews would take their aircraft for a short half-hour air test over their base; all equipment would be thoroughly tested by the crew and any last minute snags reported to the ground crew for rectification. After lunch the crews would try to kill time until they were due for briefing. All this time, of course, the willing ground staff were working hard preparing the aircraft for the night's operation. There was little to occupy the aircrews at this time. Some tried to sleep for a couple of hours, others tried to take their minds off the coming raid with games of snooker, cards or chess, but the thought of the coming operation was never far away.

Many medical officers held the opinion that it was these hours of waiting that wore into the men's nerves as much as anything that happened to them in the air. It was the contrast between the life of the station around them, itself surrounded by the afternoon peace of rural England, and the thought of what awaited them over Germany in a few hours' time, that imposed such a strain on bomber crews at this time. Looking around they could see the familiar sights; the hangars, the station staff going about their duties. It all took on a strange sense of unreality. A gunner walking to the mess might come across a WAAF girlfriend; he would explain briefly that he was unable to see her that evening but would make arrangements to meet the following day, knowing in his heart that he might well be dead that same night.

At last would come the time for briefing; they would gather together, these young men, crew by crew on the bench seats in the briefing room facing the elevated stage at the far end, the map above still hidden by a curtain, until the moment when the commanding officer pulled aside the curtain to reveal the target. The squadron commander usually conducted the briefing, and after his opening remarks the specialist officers, the bombing leader, signals leader, navigation leader, gunnery leader, engineer leader, intelligence and met officers would make their contributions.

The station commander would wish them luck, and the crews would shuffle to their feet talking to each other about the target and gathering up their notes and maps. In the crew room they would strip themselves of all personal possessions, don their flying clothing, gather their parachutes, flying rations and escape kit and board the waiting transport to take them to their aircraft. At the dispersals they would lie on the grass, smoking and chatting to the ground crew, until the time came to board their aircraft. The pilot and flight engineer ran up the engines, with the ground crew NCO watching over their shoulders; the rest of the crew would give a last minute check to their equipment. When the pilot was satisfied that everything was in order, the NCO fitter would hand him the form 700 on a clipboard; the pilot would sign that he accepted the aircraft. The fitter slipped out of the aircraft and the flight engineer reported to his pilot, 'Rear hatch closed and secure. OK to taxi.' The pilot signalled to the ground crew to remove the chocks and commenced to taxi to the end of the runway. At the end of the runway there would be a small crowd of well-wishers: WAAFs who knew some of the crews, MT drivers, ground crews, operations clerks and other personnel not otherwise engaged. Each bomber took its place at the end of the runway and waited for a 'green' from the controller's lamp. The engines were then run up to maximum boost, the brakes released and the bomber slowly rolled off down the runway to the accompaniment of cheers, waves and shouts of good luck from the well-wishers; there was undoubtedly many a silent prayer to accompany them on their way. There was now little for the station personnel to do but wait for the returning bombers; the rest was up to the crews now setting course above the base.

This was the daily routine of life in Bomber Command, a routine that would be a way of life for the next three years.

CHAPTER EIGHT

Following the devastating attack against Cologne, Harris continued for the remainder of 1942 to carry out attacks on German cities on a wide front. Although none of these raids matched the success of the Cologne attack, nevertheless they did meet with a measure of success, far more than those of 1941. The introduction of the four-engined aircraft – the Lancasters, Halifaxes and Stirlings – with their greater bombload capacities, meant that a greater weight of bombs could be dropped on Germany than previously. The change of targets to cities and centres of industrial production also meant that more bombs were achieving some damage instead of being 'wasted', as in previous years. It might be thought by the ill-informed that, once area bombing had been introduced, attacking a city became a relatively simple exercise: it was not. Until the end of the war it remained a very difficult test of navigation and bomb-aiming skills.

By August 1942 the Germans had found a method of jamming the navigation aid GEE and it was rarely available to the crews beyond 3 degrees east; however, it still remained an invaluable aid to navigation right up to the last days of the war. The scientists of the Telecommunications Research Establishment at Malvern were applying themselves to solving the navigation problems of 1940 and 1941, and the fruits of their labours would begin to come into service toward the end of the year.

Apart from the attack on Cologne, the other significant event of 1942 was the creation of the Pathfinder Force. In the attacks on Lübeck, Rostock and Cologne, Wellingtons of No.3 Group had carried out an early form of target-marking by the use of flares, followed by aircraft carrying incendiaries to start fires as aiming points for the following waves of bombers. A number of highly-experienced bomber pilots, notably such men as Charles Whitworth, Jimmy Marks and Willie Tait were, however, convinced that something more was needed to obtain a greater concentration on the target. This 'select' band and others knew some of the most experienced bomber pilots who now occupied staff posts at Air Ministry. Foremost among these was Group Captain Sydney Bufton, who now occupied the post of Director of Bomber Operations, and was the Chief of Air Staff's adviser on matters relating to bombing policy.

Ever since his days as commander of No.4 Group's 10 and 76 squadrons, Bufton had been preoccupied with the problem of target location and marking. At the Air Ministry he argued passionately for the formation of a separate force, whose function would be to locate and mark the target for the rest of the Command. Bufton eventually obtained the support and backing of the Vice Chief of Air Staff Sir Wilfred Freeman for his ideas. The concept of a separate target marking force led to one of the most bitter debates of the war between Harris and the Air Staff.

It was not that Harris was opposed in any way to the principle of selected crews leading the rest of his force: his objection was to the formation of a separate force. He considered that to take the best crews away from their squadrons and form them into a separate target-finding force would, in the long run, mean that the efficiency of his main force squadrons would suffer. Harris has, in fact, gone on record as saying that he wanted not one pathfinder force but several – one in every group! There is no doubt that Harris also objected strongly to, as he saw it, being given directions by a junior officer!

Despite the Commander in Chief's objections, a consensus of opinion at Air Ministry emerged in favour of a specialist target-finding and marking force, as opposed to Harris's idea of using selected crews from the main force squadrons to mark for his bombers. On 14 June 1942 Harris received a letter from the Chief of Air Staff Portal which virtually amounted to a direction to form a separate formation for target locating duties. The letter said that it was 'the opinion of the Air Staff that the formation of a special force with a role analogous to that of the reconnaissance battalion of an Army division would immediately open up a new field for improvement, raising the standard and thus the morale which could not fail to be reflected throughout the whole force'.

Having lost his debate with Air Ministry, and receiving a direct order to set up the new formation, Harris, as he always did when given a direct order, carried out the instructions with good grace. In fact he fought a tough battle with the Treasury to get special recognition for the Pathfinder crews, who it had now been decided would be required to undertake forty-five operations for a tour instead of the normal thirty: this was in order to utilise to the full their extra training and expertise. This was typical of Harris. He succeeded in obtaining for these crews an acting promotion in rank and the additional pay that went with this for as long as they were on operations, as well as the award of a special Pathfinder badge which was genuinely coveted by the crews.

To lead the new formation Harris chose a young Australian-born Wing Commander, Donald Bennett. He could not have selected a man better suited to the task. A first-class pilot, widely experienced in flying all types of aircraft from fighters to flying boats and heavy bombers, Bennett was a brilliant navigator without peers. Before joining Bomber Command he had been operational manager of the Atlantic Ferry, which job was itself considered an impossible one by many Service pundits; Bennett had made a great success of ferrying aircraft from America across the Atlantic to Britain, in the depth of an awful winter. After joining Bomber Command he had commanded No.4 Group's 77 and 10 Squadrons. Whilst commanding 10 Squadron he had attacked the *Tirpitz* in April 1942; Bennett was shot down on this attack, evaded capture, escaped from Norway and returned to Britain to resume operational flying.

In his book *Fortress without a Roof* the American writer Wilbur H. Morrison says, 'Most crew members didn't like this aloof young Australian and criticised Harris's choice'. This is arrant nonsense; Bennett was respected by crew members as an outstanding airman; just 32 years old he combined youth with vast and – more important – recent operational experience. This was a combination unique among his contemporary Group commanders. The objections to Donald Bennett's appointment, such as there were, came from some senior officers in the RAF; no doubt some of these individuals resented an officer of Bennett's youth, comparatively junior rank and length of service, being appointed to what was obviously going to be a post of great importance. Bennett himself could, like Harris, upset certain people with his bluntness and made no secret of his opinion that his appointment represented the end of the 'gentlemen' and the arrival of the 'players'. The crews who flew in Bennett's force greatly admired him and in Chaz Bowyer's book *Pathfinders at War* one navigator, Bill Davies, who flew 43 operations with 156 Squadron, says that, 'everyone loved him and had a great respect for his ability'. A favourite quote of the Pathfinder crews was, 'If you were not religious you thought Bennett was Christ – if you were religious you thought he was the next best thing'.

On 11 August 1942 the official order was sent from Air Ministry to Headquarters Bomber Command to create the Pathfinder Force; Harris lost no time in implementing this order and the force was formed on 15 August with its headquarters at RAF Wyton. Bennett was promoted to Group Captain to take up his new command. It comprised just four units: No.7 Squadron (Stirlings) based at Oakington; 35 Squadron (Halifaxes) at Graveley; 156 Squadron (Wellingtons) at Warboys and 83 Squadron (Lancasters) based at Wyton. A fifth squadron, No.109, was for the moment only attached to the Pathfinder Force, based at Wyton; this unit was equipped with the new twin-engined all-wooden construction aircraft – the Mosquito. Commanded by Sydney Bufton's brother Hal, this squadron was concerned with the development and testing of a new highly-secret blind-bombing radar device codenamed OBOE.

The force was directly responsible to Commander in Chief for all operational matters, but at this stage came under HQ No.3 Group for administrative purposes. On 8 January, 1943 the force became a group in its own right, No.8 (PFF) Group. Donald Bennett was promoted to Air Commodore and eventually to Air Vice-Marshal. In a letter to the Prime Minister soon after No.8 (PFF) Group was formed, Harris described Bennett as 'one of the most efficient and finest youngsters I have ever come across in the Service' – a sentiment with which Bennett's crews would wholeheartedly agree!

In the last months of 1942 the concentration of bombing improved marginally with the introduction of the Pathfinders, despite appalling weather; and the bomber crews were delighted to see the Pathfinders' markers over the targets marking the aiming point.

Although the crews approved of the concept of this new target-marking force and now had a definite aiming point for the bomb-aimers to sight on, the Pathfinders were unable to impose any great improvement in bombing accuracy for the first few months of the force's career. This was because the Pathfinders initially had a polyglot mixture of aircraft, and were equipped with no more advanced navigation or bombing aids than the main force of the Command. It was, therefore, initially virtually a Pathfinder Force in name only. The early problems of the Pathfinders gave its critics much to comment on! The saving grace was that the crews, all volunteers, selected to form the force were excellent ones; many of them being second-tour crews. The navigation standard of these crews was, in itself, responsible for the slight initial improvement in the Command's bombing concentration. There were, of course, nights when the Pathfinder Force was in error, and scattered marking meant scattered bombing by the main force. These nights were getting fewer, and the Pathfinder Force was beginning to make its immense contribution to the improved capability of Bomber Command.

Led by Hal Bufton, 109 Squadron flew the first operational trial of OBOE on 20 December 1942, and although not entirely successful, this was to be the forerunner of the greatly improved bombing accuracy of 1943. OBOE was the vital blind bombing device for which Bomber Command had been so desperately waiting. It was a sophisticated version of the system which the Luftwaffe had used over Britain in 1940; the aircraft flew along a beam laid by a ground station in England. If the pilot strayed off the beam he received a series of dots or dashes depending whether he was off to the right or left of the beam, while the aircraft remained on the beam the signal remained steady. A second beam was laid from a second ground station to intersect the first at exactly the right spot for the bombs to be released. At the point of intersection the bombs were dropped without the ground needing to be seen. In early operations with OBOE the device proved accurate to 600 yards. (This description of OBOE has been kept deliberately simple.)

The limitations with OBOE were that the Command had only two ground stations and could only control twelve aircraft an hour over the target, thus it was necessary to have heavy bombers to 'back up' the OBOE markers if there was any lapse in these during the main force's attack. The second drawback was a more serious one; because of the curvature of the earth OBOE beams had only a limited range from the ground stations in England. The beams could be laid over targets in the Ruhr but not much further east. The OBOE equipment was fitted in the new Mosquito aircraft which, being able to operate at up to 33,000 feet, were able to obtain the maximum range from it.

The other radar device which came into service at about this time was named H2S. This was the first ever airborne radar set, which provided a shadowy image of the ground on a cathode ray tube for its operator in the aircraft above. It enabled the crews to identify targets through cloud, although it would never prove the accurate blind bombing aid which OBOE was. H2S was issued initially to the Pathfinder crews, although later it came into general use in the Command, and at first it suffered considerable teething troubles. H2S worked best near large bodies of water, e.g. lakes, harbours, coastlines, etc, which showed up clearly on the receiver. Unfortunately it tended to give blurred images over large built-up urban areas.

The winter of 1942/3 saw the introduction of specially designed Target Indicators, (TI's) for the Pathfinder Force; these were varicoloured pyrotechnic projectiles that were big enough and bright enough to be seen by the bomber crews amidst the smoke and haze of a target.

Bennett worked his Pathfinder crews hard; they went often to the grindstone in exercises and mock attacks, but his hard-driving leadership paid huge dividends in the improved accuracy of the target marking and the consequent much greater accuracy of bombing by the main force. During 1943 Bennett's crews were able to achieve incredible accuracy in marking targets, and Bomber Command at last began to show what it was really capable of over Germany.

Toward the end of the war, main force Bomber Command Groups carried out their own form of pathfinding, using basic PFF force techniques, including OBOE and a later device GEE-H; this was possibly the greatest compliment paid to No.8 (PFF) Group. It has been claimed by some critics of the PFF force that this justified the view that it was a mistake to form a separate *corps d'élite*, but these critics do not take into account the many experienced crews that served in No.8 Group, the pooling of operational knowledge, the expertise that the force developed, the hard-won tactical know-how and the steady improvement in devices provided for the group by the scientists. Finally, this view does not take into account the determination of the Pathfinder crews to enable a far greater weight of bombs to be dropped on targets in Germany where the said bombs would hurt most.

The architect of this great advance in bombing efficiency was Air Vice-Marshal Donald Bennett. He may have upset some of the RAF hierarchy – and also some of the politicians – with his single-minded determination, but he changed the concept of strategic bombing; and at any one time he mustered more operational flying experience than the combined total of his contemporary group commanders.

CHAPTER NINE

B omber Command in that winter of 1942/3 saw other innovations in equipment and tactics. It was now recognised that moonlight made the vulnerable bombers easy prey to night fighters, and the Command was increasingly operating on dark moonless nights with broken cloud cover. The policy of routeing the bombers over enemy territory in a concentrated 'stream', first used on the Cologne attack, was now used for every operation: as 1943 wore on the 'stream' would become ever more concentrated and intensified. Aircraft were now being fitted with 'Monica', a device which gave warning of other aircraft approaching. Group Captain Addison's 80 Wing, which would eventually become No.100 Group, was beginning to use the first of the immense range of radio counter-measures which would eventually be employed against the German defences.

In January, 1943 a new heavy bomber group was formed, No.6 Group. This group was unique in that it was a Canadian Group; its eventual thirteen squadrons were all Royal Canadian Air Force squadrons, its commander was a Canadian officer and most of its running costs were met by Canada. Despite being a Canadian formation No.6 Group was fully integrated operationally into Bomber Command, and was under the direct operational control of Harris. This was typical of Canada's total commitment to Britain's war effort.

Harris himself wrote, 'At long last we were ready and equipped'. He has identified the start of his true onslaught on Germany as the night of 5 March 1943. At 20·58 on that night an OBOE equipped Mosquito of the Pathfinder Force dropped its target-indicator bombs where the two OBOE beams intersected in the atmosphere nearly six miles above the Krupps factory in Essen. During the next forty minutes more OBOE Mosquitoes re-marked the target; these markers were accurately backed up by other target markers dropped by the heavy bombers of the Pathfinder Force.

Over 400 aircraft of the main force accurately dropped their bombloads on the target indicators. This attack marked a major turning point in the bombing offensive: Essen, one of Germany's most vital industrial centres, had been attacked many times but had, until this night, only suffered minor damage. With its perpetual industrial haze and fierce defences it had been one of the most difficult to hit of Bomber Command's targets. But this night, for the first time, the crews did not need a clear sight of the ground. The bomb-aimers had only to aim at the accurately placed target indicators glowing clearly through the haze 20,000 feet below. The attack was a major success and the results were impressive; over 600 acres of Essen were devastated, the Krupps works were particularly badly damaged; these results were achieved for the loss of fourteen aircraft.

The winter months of attacks against Germany on a wide front were over: Harris was about to commence the first of his three great campaigns of 1943. These three campaigns, which historians have entitled 'battles'; the Battles of the Ruhr, Hamburg, and Berlin, were to make 1943 the most celebrated, the most intensive and the bloodiest year of the bomber war; the first battle, that of the Ruhr, opened at 20·58 on 5 March.

Although the historians now remember the Ruhr as one of the three great battles of 1943, the crews who fought the battle and carried out its forty-three major attacks between 5 March and 12 July had not the privilege of the historian's hindsight. The crews only knew that they flew night after night to some of the most heavily defended targets in Germany. Some of these targets, Berlin, Munich and Stuttgart, were not even in the Ruhr; targets outside the Ruhr area had to be attacked from time to time to prevent the enemy from concentrating his defence exclusively on the Ruhr. In fact, eleven more distant targets were attacked during the course of the battle; it became apparent during these raids that operations beyond the range of OBOE could not achieve the same accuracy as the Ruhr attacks, and marking of more distant targets remained a problem for the remainder of the war.

The crews did not realise until long afterwards that the tide of the air war was beginning to turn: what they did realise, even in such small and close-knit communities as the squadrons, was that the cost in lives was appalling. The familiar faces vanished from the messes: new crews arrived but the older ones seldom learned their names. Crews fully trained on the heavy bombers arrived from the Heavy Conversion Units; often they did not have time to unpack their kit fully before they were lost over the Ruhr. The crews were seldom far from their bases. To live until the next six days' leave became the goal for most of them! Few crews, at this time, reached more than nine or ten operations before they, too, were lost. The crews were briefed day after day: on some nights the weather was so bad that the operation was cancelled while they were actually in the aircraft waiting to take off. On these 'stand-down' nights there were even more frenzied, hilarious parties in the messes and the local pubs.

The briefings and the operations continued at high pressure and, with a few exceptions, the operations were all against the Ruhr. After a period the most ordinary of men can become accustomed to the most fantastic of lives. They became used to seeing bombers explode in the air around them, and to learn that in them were men they had known and liked. Most aircrew men who operated during the twelve months from March 1943 to March 1944 became reconciled to the probability that they would die on operations 'sometime' and accustomed themselves to living each day to the full. The most remarkable thing about this twelve months was that morale in the Command remained at such a high level. Many crews who did survive to complete their tour of operations and were posted to instruct at OTU or HCU, could not wait to get back on a second tour of operations and fought a constant battle with authority until they were allowed to rejoin their squadrons. For these men there was a strange compulsion to continue on operational flying; away from the life of an operational squadron they felt that there was something missing. If one asked them what it was they missed; why they were so anxious to return to operations, few would be able to give a logical answer: for these men the strange alchemy of life on an operational squadron had mixed its strongest potion.

One thing is certain: the comradeship of the men of an operational bomber crew (perhaps comradeship is not a strong enough word to describe the close ties of a good operational crew) was something that these men had never experienced before and would never encounter again in their lives; for many of them it was this relationship with their fellow crew members that drew them back to operations. Tragically, a good proportion of aircrew returning for a second tour went missing on that tour. Some men completed not two but three tours; towering even above these were legendary figures: those the public were to hear much of Gibson and Cheshire, Pickard and Edwards but also others not so well known to the public but admired and respected throughout the Command. Men such as Alec Cranswick who flew a phenomenal number of operations in heavy bombers – Don Bennett in his book *Pathfinder* credits him with 143 – Mickey Martin, Syd Clayton, Dennis Witt, Willie Tait, Hamish Mahaddie and others. These men, however, were exceptions: blessed with a rich combination of skill and luck that comes to very few. In the twelve month period between March 1943 and March 1944 the average crews in Bomber Command were lucky to manage more than a dozen operations before they were lost. Despite the grievous losses there was never any shortage of replacements and at no time was the high standard of the crews allowed to deteriorate.

Between 5 March and 12 July 1943 Bomber Command carried out forty-three major attacks on Germany, of which two-thirds were against the Ruhr. The Command had dropped 58,000 tons of bombs on Germany, more than the Luftwaffe had dropped on Britain throughout 1940 and 1941, more than Bomber Command dropped on Germany in the whole of 1942. Nine major towns in the Ruhr, Germany's main industrial centre, had been devastated, among them Essen, Duisburg, Wuppertal and Düsseldorf. Enormous damage had been done to Germany's production capacity, thousands of acres of industrial plant had been razed; many thousands had been made homeless. The Command had despatched 18,506 sorties and lost 872 aircraft; a loss rate of 4·7 per cent.

The Battle of the Ruhr had been a triumphant victory for Bomber Command, and although the price of victory had been high, the overall loss rate had remained below the five per cent figure. Within the period of time covered by the Battle of the Ruhr the famous Dams raid took place.

Much has been written about this attack and in 1955 the film *The Dam Busters* was first released. The film, which is an excellent account of the preparation for, build up to, and actual attack on, the Ruhr dams is still shown on television at quite frequent intervals. No account of Bomber Command's war could, however, omit at least a brief mention of this brilliant feat of arms.

The dams were:

(1) The Möhne – situated in the Möhne Valley, south-east of Dortmund. This dam's function was to collect rainfall to prevent winter flooding and to provide power for electrical generators. It played an essential part in sustaining underground water supply vital for industrial and household supplies.

(2) The Eder – south of Kassel and south-east of the Möhne dam. It acted as a reservoir for the Mittelland Canal, running from the Ruhr to Berlin. It prevented flooding in winter, and served hydroelectric power stations.

(3) The Sorpe, Ennepe and Lister dams –
situated south of Dortmund and south-west of
the Möhne. The function of these dams was
similar to that of the Möhne.

Barnes Wallis, the brilliant engineer and designer, who
held the post of Controller of Armament Research and
Development at Vickers Armstrong, had conceived the idea
of attacking the dams and had devised the perfect weapon: a
spherical bomb or mine, both words could be used to
describe this weapon, which would bounce along the surface
of the water, come to rest against the dam, sink below the
surface of the water and explode against the dam wall.

Barnes Wallis's bomb was sixty inches long and fifty
inches in diameter. It had three hydrostatic pistols set to
detonate at 30 feet, also a ninety second time fuse, set at
release from the aircraft, to destroy the weapon if the pistols
failed to function. The total weight of the weapon was 9,250
pounds. On each end of the cylindrical casing was a hollow
circular tract, twenty inches in diameter, into which disc-like
wheels mounted on supporting calliper arms were fitted with
fore and aft axis. A safety pin was attached to a wire which
in turn was attached to one of the calliper arms; this released
the weapon when the bomb-aimer pressed his release switch.
When activated the calliper arms holding each side of the
bomb sprang open, and away went the weapon. To obtain the
desired bounce to skim the weapon across the water it had to
be spinning in a backward rotation before release. The power
for rotating the weapon before release was provided by a
hydraulic motor with belt drive to one of the discs. The spin
was transmitted to the bomb by friction contact between the
internal tracks and the driven disc. The hydraulic motor was
started ten minutes before arrival at the target.

After much patient trial and error it had been found that
the weapon had to be released at an exact height of 60 feet,
at a speed of 240–250 miles per hour, and it had to be
released at between 400 and 500 yards from the dam wall. To

meet these requirements precision flying of the highest standard was needed.

On 15 March 1943 Sir Arthur Harris told Air Vice-Marshal Cochrane (who in 1942 had been appointed Air Officer Commanding No.5 Group) the details of Wallis's weapon and the proposed attack on the Ruhr dams, and that he intended that Cochrane's Group should undertake the attack. Both men felt that, rather than remove one of Cochrane's squadrons from the attacks on Ruhr targets, it would be preferable to form a new squadron from experienced crews in the Group. It was considered that these should be crews who had just finished or were about to finish a tour of operations. Harris and Cochrane were unanimous in their choice for command of this new squadron – Wing Commander Guy Gibson.

Gibson had just completed a tour of operations in command of 106 Squadron, and was actually looking forward to some well deserved leave, when he was ordered to report to Cochrane at 5 Group Headquarters. Cochrane asked him whether he would be prepared to do one more trip and, although he could give Gibson no details at this stage – it would be some time before Gibson knew the actual targets – the AOC stressed the vital importance of the operation. Gibson agreed to take on the task. All he knew was that he was to command a new squadron, which he was to form and lead, and for which he was to have an almost free hand in picking his pilots and crews: something no squadron commander had been allowed to do before!

The squadron, which was given the number 617, was based at RAF station Scampton. Gibson was given every assistance in his power by Charles Whitworth, who was now Scampton's station commander. The squadron began intensive training on 31st March; at 21·28 on the night of 16 May the first aircraft took off from Scampton en route to attack the Ruhr dams.

The operation was a triumph for 617 Squadron: the

Möhne and Eder dams were both breached and flood waters poured over large areas, villages and towns were flooded and the waters reached Kassel, thirty-five miles away from the Eder. Kassel was the largest tank and aircraft engine manufacturing centre in Germany. Two hundred yards of railway embankment had been destroyed at Wabern, the station sidings at Kassel were silted up and the dock railways flooded. Parts of Kassel's U-boat, tank and artillery manufacturing plants were severely affected. These were targets on which Bomber Command had made several previous attacks without causing as much damage as the flood. The main railway viaduct between Dortmund and Hagen had been severed and some thirty-two miles of countryside flooded.

This feat of arms was not attained without heavy loss; 19 Lancasters took off from Scampton, eleven returned in the early hours, eight aircraft were lost.

Wing Commander Guy Gibson received the award of the Victoria Cross for his great courage in leading the attack; a truly deserved award. Mick Martin, who himself was awarded the DSO for this attack, has said, 'He was a matchless leader and airman and no VC could have been more deserved.' In recent years some writers have tried to suggest that this attack achieved little result. In making this quite false claim these individuals only insult the memory of the young men who died on this operation. These airmen were quite outstanding youngsters who, had they survived, would undoubtedly have achieved much in their chosen careers. In attempting to decry their achievements on the night of 16 May 1943, these writers reveal themselves in their true colours.

Anyone wishing to study this attack in detail is recommended to read Paul Brickhill's *The Dam Busters*; Alan W. Cooper's *The Men who Breached the Dams*; and, for the finest descriptive writing of all, Wing Commander Gibson's own *Enemy Coast Ahead*.

Although 617 Squadron had been formed for just this one operation, Harris decided to keep the squadron in existence, and to use it in the future as a specialist squadron for attacks on selected targets. The squadron was to have a distinguished record and become the most famous squadron in the RAF; during the remainder of the Second World War a very select and distinguished company of men would serve in its ranks.

The Battle of the Ruhr ended on 14 July; before the month was over Sir Arthur Harris had already commenced the next of his major campaigns, the short, heavy and outstandingly successful series of attacks against the port of Hamburg.

Although the Command's losses during the campaign against the Ruhr had been heavy, these losses had affected the Command surprisingly little. The aircrew training programmes and the aircraft factories had more than replaced the losses. In January 1943 Bomber Command had only 483 bombers available for night operations; at the end of the Battle of the Ruhr the front-line strength stood at over 800 aircraft.

In addition to its greatly increased strength, Bomber Command was to use against Hamburg a new tactical device which would prove a major breakthrough against the German defences. In the highly technical electronics war now being waged above Germany this device was an article of utter simplicity. It was simply a piece of metal foil strip; one side aluminium foil, the other black, roughly one foot long and half an inch wide. If these strips were dropped from the bombers in sufficient quantity the slowly descending clouds produced a barrier which would 'fog' the German radar screens. Approximately two thousand of these strips produced a radar echo similar to that of a bomber. The value of this device, which was code-named 'window', had been known since the spring of 1942, but at a meeting to discuss its future use Lord Cherwell, the Prime Minister's scientific adviser, had pointed out that if it would work against German radar, then it would also be effective against Britain's.

The Ministry of Home Security, Fighter Command and Anti-Aircraft Command opposed its use by Bomber Command. By the autumn of 1942 the Luftwaffe had become a negligible threat to Britain and, ironically, the Germans had already produced a version of 'window', but they too had banned its use in case the British copied it! Fortunately, however, the enemy had not produced any window-proof radar sets. In the Official History, Webster and Frankland comment on the failure of Harris to 'exert himself to secure the introduction of a measure which was expected so greatly to favour the offence at the expense of the defence'. This is a rather curious comment for Webster and Frankland to make; Harris had been pressing urgently for the use of window and had become increasingly angry over the attitude of the Home Defence Commands which opposed its introduction. He had made strong representations to the Prime Minister about its use, pointing out that most of the Command's losses were due to radar-directed night fighters.

In July 1943 Churchill overruled the Ministry of Home Defence and Fighter Command. In typically Churchillian manner, he declared majestically, 'let us open the window'. The fact that by July 1943 a British night-fighter radar had been produced that was immune to window jamming, might have had some slight influence on the Prime Minister's decision. Once again, however, the Official Historians appear to have been less than just to Sir Arthur Harris.

On the evening of 24 July 1943, the crews of Bomber Command were briefed to take part in the heaviest attack of the war thus far, on Hamburg. Many of the crews had been to Hamburg before but this time, they were told, it would be different. First, 791 aircraft would be taking part in the attack, code-named 'Operation Gomorrah'. Secondly, this time they would be using a marvellous new device which would make it easy. It is a measure of the faith the crews now had in the scientists that they were delighted with the vision of confusion among the enemy defences. At one 4 Group station in Yorkshire, a pilot asked the pertinent question, 'Why haven't we had this before?' 'Er – a good question,' replied the briefing officer.

Hamburg was beyond the range of OBOE but, situated on a wide river and being close to the sea, it would show up clearly on H2S. The plan of campaign was a straightforward one; to bomb Hamburg until it was destroyed. The Pathfinder Force would carry out the target marking by the illumination of flares dropped by H2S equipped aircraft. Window would be the surprise that would nullify the enemy defences; the American 8th Air Force would take part with daylight attacks. If everything went as planned the fate of Hamburg was sealed.

The night of 24 July was a clear one; the bombers flew across the North Sea towards Hamburg and, at the predetermined point in the flight, the crews started dropping the strips of window. The German defences were thrown into complete disarray; their radar screens showed a fantastically impossible number of aircraft approaching their coast. The screens were completely fogged by radar echoes, if the echoes on the screens were correct then literally thousands upon thousands of British aircraft were on the way. The British aircrews were dazzled by the vision before them as they approached Hamburg, searchlights were weaving aimlessly across the sky desperately trying to illuminate a bomber, any bomber; one pilot described the searchlights as 'wandering across the sky like drunken men'. Hamburg's fifty-six heavy and thirty-six light anti-aircraft batteries were firing a blind box barrage into the night sky above the city, unable to take radar predictions on the bombers above. The radar-directed night fighters were helpless, and failed completely to locate the bomber stream. It was a moment of complete and utter triumph for the bombers in their duel against the night fighters, and the bomber crews made the most of it. The attack on Hamburg on 24 July was perfectly co-ordinated, one of the best orchestrated attacks since the war began.

A magnetic mine being loaded onto a Hampden in 1941

A flight of Wellingtons, February 1940

Air Chief Marshal Sir Ralph Cochrane CBE. KCB. AFC.

Ground crew working on a Stirling, October 1942

A Lancaster crew about to depart on a raid against Calais, 23rd September 1944

The aircrew and groundcrew of 51 squadron Halifax X-x ray (the author's aircraft) photographed in 1944

51 (B) squadron aircrew at RAF Snaith briefing for the attack on Nuremberg 30th March 1944. Six out of seventeen crews were lost on this raid, including that of S/Ldr Hill DFC, seen here conducting the briefing

Station and squadron staff at RAF Snaith awaiting the return of aircraft
after the raid on Nuremberg 30/31st March 1944

The author's crew being debriefed after returning from the Nuremberg raid on the
30/31st March 1944

Pilot Officer C. J. Barton VC.

Air Vice Marshal Donald Bennett CB. CBE. DSO

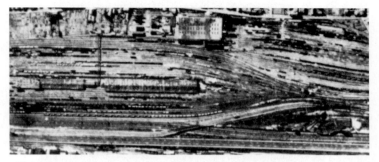

The railway yards at Juvisy-sur-Orgne, which were selected for attack as part of the Transportation Plan

The same railway yards after the Bomber Command raid of the 18/19th April 1944. The bombing accuracy achieved is clearly visible

Sir Arthur T. Harris. BT. GCB. OBE. AFC. LL. D

Zero hour, or H-hour as it was termed, was 01·00. Two minutes before H-hour twenty Pathfinder aircraft dropped yellow Target Indicators blind on H2S, under ideal conditions, since Hamburg's coastline gave an exceptionally sharp radar image. They were followed by eight Pathfinders who dropped red TIs visually. During the course of the attack these markers were backed up with green TIs dropped visually by a further fifty-three Pathfinders. The main force bombed the markers from H-hour plus 2 minutes to H-hour plus 48 minutes. The attack was an overwhelming success. Of the bombing photographs the crews brought back, 306 showed bombs dropped within a circle of three miles of the aiming point. Vast areas of Hamburg were utterly devastated; only twelve aircraft failed to return from the 791 despatched. The next morning the people of Northern Germany awoke to find metal foil strips littered across the countryside, like Christmas decorations, hanging from telephone wires and draped across hedges, houses and farms. The German scientists knew what these strips were; they fully understood the use of window; their masters had refused to use it for the same reasons as Harris's masters. At the moment the Germans had no answer to the use of window.

In daylight on 25 and 26 July the 8th Air Force flew 235 sorties to Hamburg to stoke up the fires started by Bomber Command.

In *Fortress Without a Roof* Morrison says, 'The 8th Air Force did not join the Royal Air Force in bombing the city, concentrating instead on the dock areas in daylight, although some American bombs were jettisoned on the city by crippled bombers'. He goes further, and says, 'The British must accept responsibility for the destruction of Hamburg'.

The kindest thing that can be said about the first statement is that Morrison has made a factual error; perhaps he has been misled by the American Official History and the United States Strategic Bombing Survey which unfortunately erected a smokescreen of careful concealment of the

American part in the area bombing campaign. This attitude on the part of the American historians, like that of a lot of British politicians, is far less straightforward, and indeed much less attractive, than Sir Arthur Harris's open commitment and frank honesty concerning the true nature of area bombing. Unfortunately, since the war many people have laboured under the mistaken impression that it was Bomber Command alone that was responsible for the area bombing of German cities.

Concerning the second statement; Bomber Command has never attempted to evade responsibility for the destruction of Hamburg, and no-one in any position of authority in Bomber Command has ever attempted to conceal the true nature of area bombing.

On the night of 25 July Mosquito aircraft staged a light nuisance raid on Hamburg, to further worry and exhaust the defences and air-raid services. Then on 27 July, Bomber Command returned in force, despatching 787 aircraft; of these a total of 722 claimed to have bombed Hamburg. On 29 July the Command attacked again, this time 777 aircraft being sent against the city: the final attack was on the night of 2 August by 740 aircraft which carried out the operation in appalling weather. This last operation was not completely successful, due to the conditions, but the Battle of Hamburg had already been won by Bomber Command.

On the night of 27 July, the second attack, a terrible firestorm engulfed the city. As the multitude of fires in Hamburg gradually got out of control they merged into an awful inferno. The temperature in the fire reached fantastic figures – 1,000 degrees Centigrade and more – the fires sucked in air and billowed into hurricanes of fire and smoke that tore through the centre of Hamburg at 150 mph. Stocks of coal and coke fuelled the fires from the cellars of every house in their path. Thousands were suffocated in the cellars in which they had taken refuge, their bodies were incinerated where they died. Air-raid shelters became vast crematoria.

Approximately 50,000 people were estimated to have been killed and over 40,000 injured. 580 factories, 76 public buildings, 83 banks, 12 bridges, 40,358 houses, 275,000 flats, 2,632 shops, 277 schools, 58 churches and 24 hospitals had been totally obliterated. One million refugees fled the city. Hamburg was, at dawn on August 3, a smoking ruin: an empty city 'sunk in a great silence of death', according to contemporary German reports.

Within the space of ten nights and nine days from 24 July to 3 August, Hamburg had suffered four massive RAF night attacks and two daylight attacks by the American 8th Air Force. In this short space of time the Allied bombers had killed more people than the Luftwaffe killed in Britain by air-raids during the entire war. Hamburg temporarily ceased to exist as a city.

The Nazi leadership was profoundly shaken by the Battle of the Ruhr and the destruction of Hamburg. Speer said that after the Ruhr and Hamburg he realised, for the first time, that Germany was going to lose the war. Albert Speer, the Reichminister for Armaments, also recorded in his memoirs that if Bomber Command had followed up the attack on Hamburg with similar attacks on other cities, Germany would not have been able to withstand them and would have had to capitulate. In the event the Command did not follow up these attacks with the same severity or weight until 1945. No doubt if the Command had been able to do so, the same writers who have denigrated Harris and the Command in recent years would have been even more hysterical in their attacks and accused Bomber Command of terrorising the enemy into surrender.

Bomber Command was unable to follow up the attack against Hamburg with similar attacks in 1943 for some very good and logical reasons. Hamburg was in north Germany and required a relatively short penetration into enemy night fighter defence. Those major cities which the Command had not attacked lay deep inside Germany. The enemy could always mount a formidable resistance against attack on these cities if they were aware of the target; which they would have been if the Command had attempted a Hamburg-style campaign against them. In this event the losses to the Command would have been prohibitive. It is easy for critics to criticise the Command for what they claim was a failure to follow up the Hamburg attack. Harris and his staff did not, unfortunately, have the benefit of hindsight that an armchair critic has from a distance of some forty to fifty years. A point these individuals might consider is that in the first attack on 24 July Bomber Command lost twelve aircraft, from the second on 27 July seventeen aircraft failed to return and thirty bombers were lost on both the 29 July and 2 August raids. Despite the enemy defences being thrown into confusion by the use of window, the Germans had quickly improvised the use of fighters, many of them single-engined fighters, which were vectored onto the bomber stream by radio running commentary as information came in from observation posts along the bombers' route.

The Luftwaffe responded to window with remarkable speed and flexibility, assisted by their scientists' instant understanding of the crisis. They realised that, overnight, the radar-controlled interception of individual bombers had been eclipsed. Only a matter of weeks before, the Luftwaffe had created the first 'Wild Boar' units; these were single-engined fighter squadrons which were vectored onto the bomber stream by a radio commentary. Information on the British bombers' direction and changes of course were sent into central control rooms from observation posts all over Germany. Following the Hamburg raids these units were immediately reinforced. The 'Wild Boars' became the basis of the Luftwaffe counter-offensive, and formidable they proved, although suffering heavy loss from accidents.

Urgent measures were put in hand by the Germans to equip more night-fighter squadrons with their own airborne radar sets, which the Luftwaffe hoped would be able to overcome some of the problems caused by window. The air war over Germany was becoming increasingly complex; an electronic battle of measure and counter-measure.

The situation on 3 August 1943, was that Sir Arthur Harris had mounted two major campaigns against the enemy, and had won a major victory in both offensives.

'It is my firm belief that we are on the verge of a final showdown in the bombing war, and that the next few months will be vital'; thus wrote Sir Arthur Harris to Chief of Air Staff Sir Charles Portal on 12 August 1943. Bomber Command had won the first two battles of 1943; now, with the approach of the longer nights, Harris intended to mount a major offensive against the capital of Germany – Berlin – the target Bomber Command called the 'Big City'.

The third great battle of 1943 would shortly begin.

CHAPTER TEN

In January 1943 Roosevelt and Churchill held the Casablanca conference at which the directors of the American and British war effort discussed and decided upon their future strategy. Once the major strategic decision of the conference had been taken; that the invasion of Northern Europe would take place in 1944, and not before, it was obvious that the Allies would continue to press on with the bombing offensive against Germany.

It was agreed at this conference that the Combined Bomber Offensive, as it would in future be termed, should be 'to weaken Germany's war-making capacity to the point to which invasion would become possible'. The opening phrase of the directive – CCS 166/I/D from the Combined Chiefs of Staff to Air Marshal Harris and General Eaker (the Commander of the 8th Air Force) reads:

'Your primary aim will be the progressive destruction and dislocation of the German military, industrial and economic system, and the undermining of the morale of the German people to a point where their capacity for armed resistance is fatally weakened...'

In the months following the Casablanca conference an operational committee produced what was termed the Eaker Plan, intended to form the Directive into realistic orders for the 8th Air Force and Bomber Command. The Eaker Plan reflected some of General Eaker's thinking: if the 8th Air Force could be built up to 2,702 aircraft by 1 April 1944, Eaker promised that German submarine construction could be reduced by 80 per cent, fighter construction by 43 per cent, bomber construction by 65 per cent, ball bearings by 76 per cent, synthetic rubber production by 50 per cent. 'These figures,' the General claimed, 'are conservative and can be absolutely relied upon.' Harris's critics have over the years

made many disparaging comments on statements made by
the Air Marshal, but few similar comments have been offered
on the wildly optimistic American claims.

The Eaker Plan continued:

'This plan does not attempt to prescribe the major effort
of the RAF Bomber Command. It simply recognises the fact
that when precision targets are bombed by the 8th Air Force
in daylight, the effort should be complemented by RAF
bombing attacks against the surrounding industrial area at
night. Fortunately the industrial areas which the British
Bomber Command has selected for mass destruction
anyway...'

This plan was endorsed by Portal and Harris in April
1943, with only reservations about the prominence given to
the submarine bases on the French coast, which had already
proved virtually invulnerable to bombing.

At Casablanca it had been decided that the Chiefs of
Staffs' authority for the Combined Bomber Offensive should
be nominally vested in Sir Charles Portal. In Washington
General Arnold, the Head of the USAAF, was unhappy about
this arrangement. On 22 April 1943 Arnold wrote to Portal:

'It occurs to me that the time has arrived for the
establishment of somewhat more than formalised machinery
for the closest possible co-ordination, or rather integration, of
the two bomber efforts. The increasing complexity of their
operations would appear to me as soon to be beyond the
capabilities of the commanders, in person, to co-ordinate.'

This was the first of many notes from Arnold along the
same lines. Harris, with his experience as Head of the RAF
Delegation in Washington, was the first to recognise
American attempts to incorporate Bomber Command in
some joint Allied command structure which the Americans
obviously intended should be American dominated.

At this stage of the war Bomber Command was Britain's
last entirely independent contribution to the Allied war effort,
and as such it gripped the imagination of the British people

and most of the peoples of Occupied Europe. Both Portal and Harris looked upon the Casablanca directive as a general mandate for the bomber offensive, and not a specific instruction which had to be strictly obeyed to the letter. Some staff officers at Air Ministry were impressed by the American concept of daylight precision bombing, and sought to press their views on Portal. The Chief of Air Staff and Harris were not impressed, however. They considered, rightly, that self-defending bomber formations, however heavily armed, would be unable to venture far over Germany without heavy loss. Harris and his staff at High Wycombe looked upon the Casablanca directive as authorisation to continue along the course they were already pursuing and at this stage, at any rate, Portal agreed with Harris.

In May 1943, the final proposals based on Casablanca and General Eaker's Plan came before the Washington summit conference; on 10 June the final directive entitled 'Pointblank' was formally issued to the 8th Air Force and Bomber Command. The American airmen got what they wanted: orders to develop the daylight precision bombing campaign. Portal and Harris both considered they received authority to proceed with their onslaught on the urban areas of Germany.

The American commanders addressed themselves to their task with unbounded hope, and the 8th Air Force crews with great determination and courage attempted to carry out their commanders' orders. Tragically the crews soon learned the same lessons their British comrades had learned earlier: the Luftwaffe could wreak terrible destruction on unescorted bomber formations in daylight. After a short period the American bombers had to operate as far as possible with fighter escort.

The Americans also suffered another disappointment in their efforts. On 27 August 1942, General Eaker had predicted that 40 per cent of his aircraft's bombs would be dropped within five hundred yards of the aiming point, and that he would be able to pick off precision targets at will.

General Spaatz, his immediate superior, endorsed Eaker's enthusiasm. The USAAF's great bubble of optimism and enthusiasm, which mirrored that of the RAF's at the beginning of the war, would be brutally burst within a year. To an uncommitted observer it was clear, from the early American operations in the autumn of 1942, that the hopes of their commanders would be dashed. In these attacks the 8th Air Force had done some slight damage to the targets, but their bombs had also been scattered on the French civilian population in an alarming manner. The much vaunted Norden bombsight, which the press in America claimed could 'put a bomb in a pickle barrel from 20,000 feet', may have been very impressive in the clear summer skies over Nebraska or Texas, but it was virtually useless in the almost perpetual overcast European skies.

It was not long before the Americans were reduced to blind bomb-aiming through cloud using H2X, the American name for the British device H2S. The British, realising the difficulty their American colleagues were facing, had placed supplies of this device at their disposal, although Bomber Command desperately needed all the sets it could get hold of to equip its main force bombers. While Harris fought his great battles at night, and made no attempt to conceal from the press or public the nature of area bombing, the USAAF in the winter of 1943/4 was forced to turn to area bombing. That winter, using H2X to bomb blind through cloud, the 8th Air Force achieved an average circular error of some 2 to 3 miles from the aiming point; this was comparable to the accuracy of the RAF at night. In the American Official History the historians say, 'It seemed better to bomb low-priority targets frequently, even with less than precision accuracy, than not to bomb at all.' It would seem that the American historians have used less than precision accuracy themselves in attempting to conceal the American involvement in area bombing!

Lest anyone should think that, in stating these facts, there is any attempt to denigrate the 8th Air Force or its magnificent aircrews, let them disabuse themselves of this idea. The USAAF did not turn to area bombing until it was clear that their attempt at precision bombing was unsuccessful. In August 1943 the 8th had begun to discover that their self-defending formations could not survive over Germany against fighter attack. For two months the commanders persisted in trying to hit precision targets with these formations, the crews suffering terrible losses in the process.

On 17 August, 60 aircraft were lost from 376 that attacked Schweinfurt and Regensburg; on 10 October, 30 from 274 sent against Munster and, finally, on 14 October, 60 bombers were lost from 291 despatched against the ball-bearing plants at Schweinfurt. No-one could accuse the Americans of not having tried to carry out precision daylight attacks, but after the 14 October attack on Schweinfurt the 8th Air Force was forced to stop attacks beyond the range of existing Allied daylight fighters until long-range fighter escort could be provided for their bomber formations.

Such a long-range fighter was, fortunately, on the way; the P51B Mustang. This, together with the Spitfire, was one of the great fighter aircraft of the Second World War. The Mustang had originally been ordered from its American makers by the RAF in 1940. At this time the USAAF had shown little interest in the fighter. The reason was the aircraft's lack of power. When the first deliveries of the Mustang arrived in 1942 the RAF were also disappointed by the lack of power from the aircraft's Allison engine. Rolls Royce tried an experiment, replacing the Allison engine with one of their Merlins. After various modifications the RAF found themselves testing an aircraft that most designers and airmen had thought impossible, with the range to fly deep into Germany, equipped with disposable fuel tanks and, with a speed of 455 mph at 30,000 feet, the ability to outperform any German fighter.

When America needed to build up its own air forces the

Packard company began building Rolls Royce Merlin engines under licence, and a massive programme was commenced to equip the USAAF with this remarkable hybrid fighter. A satisfactory drop-tank was eventually developed and, in the spring of 1944, the Mustangs became a powerful and formidable element of the 8th Air Force.

On 6 January 1944 there was a change of command in the 8th Air Force. General Eaker was replaced by General James H. Doolittle. Doolittle was not a career USAAF officer, but had a distinguished background in both service and civilian aviation. It was Doolittle who had led the American bombing raid on Tokyo, when Mitchell B25 aircraft took off from the carrier *Hornet* and bombed the Japanese capital, a feat many airmen had thought impossible.

Doolittle used the new Mustang fighters brilliantly. He sent his bomber formations against targets the Germans were forced to defend, commencing with the massive effort against aircraft factories beginning on 20 February 1944, an effort the American press termed 'Big Week'.

Doolittle was not too bothered about the precision of his bombers: his aim was to force the Luftwaffe into the air to defend vital targets. He succeeded brilliantly; the skies over Germany were strewn day after day with the plunging wrecks of broken fighters and bombers, the black puffs of anti-aircraft bursts, the trails of rockets fired by German fighters, and among it all the glinting wings of the B17 and B24 bomber formations cruising steadily on toward the target. The battles over Germany raged for hours, successive waves of Luftwaffe fighters landing, rearming, refuelling and taking off to engage the Americans again and again. The 8th Air Force was winning a great victory over Germany. The back of the German fighter force was broken by the 8th in these air battles. The battles were fought at great cost to the American pilots and crews, but the American airmen who gave their lives in these savage battles did not make the sacrifice in vain. In winning this magnificent victory, albeit at such great cost in human life and suffering, the 8th Air Force was achieving the dominance over the Luftwaffe that would enable the USAAF and RAF to wield absolute supremacy in the air over Europe.

This book is a personal viewpoint of Bomber Command's offensive against Germany and, as such, is not the appropriate place to examine the USAAF's campaign. However this chapter has tried to correct a false impression that gained credence since the war years, principally by some American writers, that the 8th Air Force only practised precision bombing and refused to join in Bomber Command's area bombing campaign. Secondly, to pay tribute to the incredible courage and heroism of the 8th Air Force pilots and aircrews; Sir Arthur Harris himself described these crews as 'Amongst the bravest of the brave'. No aircrew member who served with Bomber Command would disagree with that statement; Bomber Command crews had nothing but the greatest admiration for the aircrews of the 8th Air Force, and regarded them as brothers-in-arms.

CHAPTER ELEVEN

Commencing in August 1943 and continuing until late November, Bomber Command embarked upon a series of attacks on more distant targets; some historians have titled these attacks 'The Road to Berlin', a rather strange nomenclature since the majority of these targets lay some considerable distance from the German capital. Included among these targets were the cities of Munich, Nuremberg and Mannheim. Some damage was caused to these targets, although not as much as High Wycombe had hoped. The Command did, however, learn a great deal from these deep penetrations into enemy territory.

The 'Wild Boar' fighters which the Luftwaffe used with some success immediately after Hamburg, were soon replaced by the 'Tame Boars'. The difficulties of operating single-engined fighters at night, without blind-flying equipment, were proving enormous and losses from accidents in night landings were becoming prohibitive. The 'Tame Boars' were twin-engined fighters, BF 110s and JU 88s, which took off to orbit a visual beacon as soon as the approximate course of the British bombers was ascertained. Bomber Command had by now discovered that the enemy could predict a raid by monitoring wireless operators' test signals during the morning air test over the bomber bases, and 100 Group accordingly broadcast fake test signals on days when the Command was not operating.

As the British bombers flew across Europe, the ground controllers directed the 'Tame Boar' fighters into the bomber stream by means of radio running commentary. The fighters then searched for the bombers on their own airborne radar sets; at this time in 1943 the Luftwaffe was still using the A1 radar, but in early 1944 the fighters were equipped with the Lichtenstein SN2 sets, which were impervious to window jamming.

At the end of August 1943, Bomber Command sent three attacks against Berlin in one week; bombing results were, however, disappointing and 7·2 per cent of the aircraft despatched were lost from these raids. Losses of this sort could not be borne for such poor results and the Berlin attacks were stopped temporarily, to await the re-equipment of the Pathfinders with improved H2S equipment, and also to devise improved tactics for deep penetration attacks.

It would be as well here to describe the type of attack the Command evolved during this period. The British tactical advance of the preceding months and the enemy response were such that the attacks of this period bore very little resemblance to earlier raids, and the late 1943 pattern attack lasted throughout the Battle of Berlin period right up to the end of March 1944.

At this time Bomber Command was mounting a major attack against Germany on average twice a week; the Command had the potential to undertake more frequent operations but it no longer operated on moonlit nights. Moonlit nights were ideal for the Luftwaffe night fighters and the Command now operated only on the dark nights, relying on their electronic devices for navigation, target marking and bombing. There was, therefore, a lull in operations during the moon period of the month and intensive attacks during the dark nights. A typical attack of this period would involve between 600 and 700 bombers capable of delivering between 2,000 and 2,500 tons of bombs.

The 'stream' first used on Cologne in 1942 was still the method of routeing the aircraft. It had been discovered that the risk of collision was not high, and the stream had been increasingly condensed. The bombers took off from their bases in the eastern counties of England and the bomber stream assembled as each aircraft, at its allotted time and height, flew over a predetermined position. By the time the enemy coast was reached the stream was complete, a swarm of aircraft approximately 70 miles long and 4,000 feet deep. The width of the stream depended on the accuracy of the navigation. It was strongly, and frequently, impressed on the crews that the concentration of the stream and their own safety depended on keeping well tucked in to the bomber stream.

The biggest problem for the bomber crews, apart from evading Luftwaffe night fighters, continued to be accurate navigation. It was important not only that the crews should find the target, but that they should adhere rigidly to the meticulous timing of the operation. If a bomber arrived too early at the target it could lead to premature disclosure of the target to the enemy; if too late the crew could find that the Pathfinders' markers had burned out, and that they had also lost the protection of the stream. The strength and direction of the wind was the important factor in accurate navigation. Predicted winds given to navigators before take-off were very often no more than a rough guide and, to obtain accurate winds while in flight, the navigators had to obtain regular 'fixes' of their position. This was not easy for only about twenty-five per cent of the main force was, at this time, equipped with H2S and the enemy often successfully jammed GEE.

Two methods were used to attempt to keep the stream concentrated; Pathfinder aircraft dropped target indicators as 'route markers' at selected points along the route to rally any aircraft wandering off track, and experienced crews with H2S were selected to act as 'Windfinders'. The navigators of these crews would keep the wireless operators informed of their calculated wind strength and direction and the wireless operators would transmit these back to England in code every half hour. These winds were averaged at Bomber Command HQ and fifteen minutes later the average was broadcast, again in code, to the whole of the force, whose navigators would use this until the next Broadcast Wind was received half an hour later.

The Luftwaffe night fighter controllers during the latter part of 1943 concentrated on the defence of the actual target, and made their main effort at that point. Bomber Command's answer was to concentrate the bombing even further. The ninety minute attack on Cologne of 1942 was now concentrated into thirty minutes or even less.

One of the most dramatic transformations of the bomber war at this time was the way both sides turned night into day. After years of darkness over blacked-out Europe, dazzling firework displays now exploded over Germany. The Pathfinder Force dropped flares to illuminate the target for their marker aircraft, whilst above the bombers the Luftwaffe were dropping lanes of flares to illuminate the British aircraft for their fighters. On nights when Bomber Command was bombing blind through cloud, the German searchlights were trained on the base of the cloud, turning the cloud into a layer of light against which the bombers were silhouetted for the fighters. One aircrew member has described the scene over the target as 'like a crazy fairground wheeling and sparkling in a mad holiday,' and the bombing run over the target as 'a tortured tumbrel ride, with flash and flare exploding in the eyes'.

Flying ahead of the main force were two groups of Pathfinder aircraft; the Illuminators who dropped masses of flares, and the Visual Markers who attempted to place their target markers on the aiming-point by the light of these flares. If visibility was good enough for this then the most accurate form of target marking, code named 'Newhaven' had been achieved: the main force would find a mass of target indicators cascading around the aiming point. These markers would be backed up by further Pathfinder aircraft for as long as the attack lasted. Conditions over the target were, however, rarely clear enough for this visual marking: haze, fog or thin scattered cloud would mean that, instead of the indicators being dropped visually, the marker crews had to drop their target indicators by H2S. The code name for this type of marking was 'Parramatta'.

When the target was covered by thick cloud the target indicators would not be visible to the main force crews, and the whole of the marking had to be carried out by the use of coloured flares attached to parachutes. The sky-markers, as they were called, had to be placed at a point in the sky in such a way that the main force's bombs would pass through that point and hit the target below: this method had the code name 'Wanganui'. This method was the most unsatisfactory of all; it was most difficult for the Pathfinder crews to execute this type of marking, even in calm conditions, and in windy conditions the sky markers were blown off this aerial aiming point almost as soon as their parachutes opened. 'Wanganui' often resulted in scattered and inaccurate bombing, but it was much better than the main force attempting to bomb blindly and indiscriminately through cloud.

The route to the target was carefully planned: in fact, routeing developed into something of an art. The route was so planned as to conceal from the enemy, until the last possible moment, the actual target. The bomber stream would 'feint' at a nearby city, if possible, and then at the last moment make a large change of course to head for the real target. En route to the target various changes of course and 'dog-legs' would be incorporated to further fox the defenders. Diversionary mine-laying operations would be laid on; these 'gardening' crews would approach the enemy coast at a considerable distance from the main force and drop large quantities of window to simulate a large bomber force approaching the coast. Along the main stream's course Mosquito aircraft of the Pathfinder Force would turn away from the main force and carry out a 'spoof' attack on a nearby city. These Mosquitoes would drop vast quantities of window, mark the city with target markers and further Mosquitoes of Bennett's Pathfinder Force would drop 4,000 lb. bombs on the decoy target. The object of these diversions was to enable the main force to get over the target and bomb before coming under attack from the Luftwaffe night-fighter force.

The Luftwaffe had five Divisional control rooms. The Germans called these control rooms 'Battle Opera Houses';

it was these control points that vectored the fighters into the bomber stream by radio running commentary. Bomber Command went to great lengths to jam these centres. No. 101 Squadron carried German speaking radio operators whose job it was to listen out for the enemy controllers and then jam their voices with a special transmitter. The code name for this was 'Airborne Cigar' or ABC for short. 101's Lancasters carried a normal full bombload and were part of the main force. All aircraft carried a small transmitter fitted near one of the engines which was switched on when orders to night fighters were being broadcast.

In addition to all the efforts by the bombers themselves, help was also given by Mosquito night fighters who carried out 'intruder' attacks on known night-fighter airfields within range of the bombers' route. Later in the Battle of Berlin period 'Serrate' Mosquitoes came into use: 'Serrate' was a radar which could home onto the German airborne radar sets carried by the Luftwaffe night fighters in 1943.

These, then, were the tactics employed by Bomber Command during late 1943 and early 1944: each nightly attack on a German city was much more than an air-raid; each attack could be described as a miniature battle. The uncomplicated bomber raids of 1940 and 1941 had developed into carefully-planned, highly-complex operations with the skies over Germany full of aircraft, heavily laden bombers opposed to fast moving night fighters; the aircraft all emitting electronic transmissions; these transmissions being echoed, reflected, received and homed upon. The bombing war had now become an intricate war of technology, with nightly battles that often resulted in the loss of a large number of lives.

There was a huge British monitoring station at Kingsdown in Kent, where fluent German speaking men and women broadcast false instructions to the German night fighters. The Luftwaffe tried playing selected music as a code to direct their fighter pilots, but the staff at Kingsdown immediately matched that ploy. As the Luftwaffe controllers changed their frequencies and strengthened the transmissions, the British matched that too!

On the night of 18 August, a further refinement was added to the Command's tactics when 597 aircraft were despatched against the V-weapon research establishment at Peenemunde. The crews were told at briefing that this was a vital 'radio location and testing site', and that if they failed to destroy it they would be sent back again and again until it was destroyed. Group Captain John Searby was appointed to act as Master of Ceremonies or, as it later became known, Master Bomber. The job of the Master Bomber was to guide the crews over the targets; instructing them which were the most accurately placed markers, ordering them to ignore inaccurate markers, calling on the marker crews to put down more markers as required; in short, to act as a general co-ordinator and director of the bombing over the target. The use of a Master Bomber would eventually become an integral part of Bomber Command attacks.

At Peenemunde the marking was exceptionally accurate; the crews made their attacks after a timed run from an offshore island to the target, and the bombing concentration was exceptional. Widespread damage was caused to the laboratories, workshops and the scientists' living quarters. The night fighters were diverted to Berlin by a well executed Mosquito 'spoof' and only managed to catch up with the last wave of the attack; even so, forty bombers were lost. The attack on Peenmunde, however, considerably delayed German production of the V-weapons, and the crews were not required to attack the site again.

During the period from the ending of the Battle of Hamburg to November, Sir Arthur Harris made a number of statements which made clear his hopes and intentions for the winter of 1943/1944. He first announced to the press that he planned a great winter campaign: then, on 3 November, in a letter to Prime Minister Churchill, he made the statement with which his critics would hound him for the rest of his life. 'We can wreck Berlin from end to end if the USAAF will come in on it. It will cost us between 400 and 500 aircraft. It will cost Germany the war.'

The 8th Air Force did not 'come in on it'. They were, in fact, in no position to do so following their heavy losses against Schweinfurt and Regensburg. Until they received supplies of the long-range Mustang, the 8th were virtually grounded, at least as far as deep penetration attacks were concerned.

Harris, therefore, went it alone; on 18 November 1943 Bomber Command embarked on the long series of deep penetration attacks that historians have titled the Battle of Berlin. In reality this was not a single assault on the German capital but a convenient title for historians to give to a struggle embracing targets all over Germany. The period from 18 November 1943 to the night of 30/31 March 1944 was, however, to be one of the bloodiest in the whole of Bomber Command's war.

CHAPTER TWELVE

On 18 November 1943 No.4 Group's station at Snaith, South Yorkshire was the home base for No.51 Squadron. The airfield was situated midway between Goole and Pontefract, south of the A645 road; wedged between the A645 to the north, the Knottingley and Goole Canal and the main London North Eastern Railway to the west, the small hamlet of Pollington lay just to the south-east corner of the airfield, and because of this many local people referred to the airfield by the hamlet's name. It was officially named after the small town of Snaith which lay to the north east of the airfield. The nearest town of any size was Selby.

RAF Snaith was one of the temporary wartime airfields that had been hastily built as Bomber Command's expansion commenced. It became operational in July, 1941 as part of No.1 Group, and was originally the home base of No.150 Squadron; this unit operated from Snaith with Wellington Mk. IIIs until October 1942. In that month Snaith was transferred to the aegis of No.4 Group and No.51 Squadron took up residence.

No.51 Squadron had a long history with the RAF: it was first formed in May 1916 as a home defence unit for defence against Zeppelin raids, deployed to defend the Midlands and London against raids approaching from the area of the Wash. It was disbanded on 13 June 1919. It was re-formed, as part of Bomber Command, on 5 March 1937 at RAF Driffield, and was equipped with Virginia and Anson aircraft. In February 1938 it received Whitley aircraft.

From the first days of the Second World War 51 Squadron had been engaged in operational flying against the enemy. The squadron was employed on the early leaflet dropping sorties over Germany until May 1940, when the Germans invaded France and the Low Countries. It then played its part in the attacks on the concentration of enemy landing craft along the Channel coast, and took part in the early struggles over Germany in 1941.

In February 1942 when its commander was Wing Commander Percy Charles Pickard, one of the legendary figures of the RAF, the squadron dropped a total of 119 paratroopers from its twelve Whitleys to carry out the raid on a German radar installation at Bruneval in France. Up until May 1942 the squadron was stationed at the 4 Group station at Dishforth in Yorkshire, but in that month it was one of the squadrons Bomber Command was forced to detach on loan to Coastal Command. Transferred to Chivenor in Devon the squadron did sterling work patrolling the Bay of Biscay until it was returned to Bomber Command in October 1942. Once again part of its parent group, No.4 Group, it was based at Snaith to re-equip with the Halifax Mk. II aircraft.

Since the squadron's return to Bomber Command it had played a prominent part in the Command's offensive over Germany, and taken part in all the attacks against the enemy; it had been particularly active in the Battles of the Ruhr and Hamburg and was now to play its part in the Battle of Berlin.

The public has heard much since the war years of the work of the RAF's 'glamour' squadrons; for example the brilliant attacks carried out by 617 Squadron, but little attention has been paid to the ordinary front-line main force squadrons. No.51 was typical of these squadrons, although it had its fair share of members who became well known to the public; among them Pickard and Willie Tait, who was to lead the attack which sank the *Tirpitz*. Toward the end of 1943 among the squadron pilots was a quiet, unassuming young man named Cyril Barton, known to many of the aircrews by the nickname 'Joe'. In some extraordinary way the squadron seemed to attract more than its fair share of 'characters', indeed, some could even be called eccentrics.

In November 1943, the squadron was commanded by a popular and much loved personality, Wing Commander Wilkerson. Wilkerson was one of the thousands of aircrew who would not survive the war, being killed while commanding 51's sister squadron No.578 at the nearby station of Burn. A previous popular commander was Wing Commander Tom Sawyer, who had been promoted to Group Captain and was Station Commander at Burn. Tom Sawyer has written an excellent book *Only Owls and Bloody Fools Fly at Night,* his personal memoirs of the war years in Bomber Command. In this book he describes some of the 'characters' he encountered in his days as 51's commander; this book is certainly recommended reading for any reader interested in Bomber Command.

On 18 November 1943, the aircrews of 51 attended briefing in the usual way: the briefing officer's opening words were 'Gentlemen, tonight your target is Mannheim. A force of 395 aircraft will attack Mannheim, while at the same time 440 bombers will carry out a heavy attack on the Big City'. As far as the crews were concerned it was to be just another deep penetration into the German defences; they did not know they were about to embark upon a long bitter struggle from which few would survive.

The television journalist Max Hastings has written a book entitled *Bomber Command,* a publication which received much acclaim from literary circles – but little from Bomber Command survivors. Hastings says that the Halifaxes were removed from the Battle of Berlin after a few weeks, and that the battle was fought by the Lancasters. This statement must have come as something of a surprise to the survivors of No.51 Squadron, and their colleagues in the rest of 4 Group, who flew their Halifax aircraft through the entire battle from 18 November to 30 March.

Between the attack on Berlin on the night of 18 November and the attack against Nuremberg on 30 March 1944, the Command launched 9,111 sorties against the German capital and 11,113 sorties against other major cities such as Stuttgart, Frankfurt, Mannheim, Leipzig, Brunswick, Schweinfurt and Nuremberg. The losses amounted to 5·1 per cent of all sorties despatched. This figure represented a total of 1,047 aircraft lost; more than the entire front-line strength of the Command. A further 1,682 aircraft were written off or badly damaged. The crews' chances of survival during this period were slim indeed.

During this period No.51 Squadron was losing a steady one or two aircraft on every operation, sometimes as many as three or four. Once again, however, morale remained remarkably high in the Command, and particularly so on 51 Squadron.

It was at the end of November 1943 that there arrived on the squadron a crew who soon began to be noticed by their fellow crews. This was not because of any particular deeds of valour or distinction; far from it! What made other crews sit up and take notice were the remarkable take-offs and landings of this particular crew's pilot. He seemed to disdain the use of most of the runway, hauling the aircraft off the ground about half to two-thirds of the way along: the landings consisted of an initial touch-down, followed by at least a further three or four – just to make sure!

Fellow crews began laying odds on this crew surviving a tour of operations: there were not many backers, even among the most inveterate gamblers. When asked about his skipper's peculiarities the rear-gunner was heard to reply, 'Oh, it doesn't worry us. We are used to him'.

On one occasion Vic Scott, the squadron bombing leader, happened to see this pilot land with an even more pronounced hop, skip and jump than usual; turning to the flying control officer Vic asked in utter astonishment 'Who the hell was that?' 'Need you ask,' came the reply.

It was not long before the squadron nicknamed the crew, 'The Flying Circus'. This name, obviously originally one of amused derision soon turned, however, into one of affectionate respect. On their third operation with the squadron, a Berlin raid, they were twice attacked by a night fighter on the way into the target. Not only did they beat off the attacks, but came home without the fighter's cannon shells having scored a hit on their aircraft. It so happened that on this trip their own bomb-aimer was in sick bay with a heavy cold so a replacement bomb-aimer flew the operation. His description of the crew discipline during the fighter attacks, and his awed description of the pilot's operational flying abilities, rapidly resulted in all bets on their survival being cancelled.

This particular crew not only fought right through the period of the Battle of Berlin, but completed their tour of operations with every member of the crew a commissioned officer and a total of five Distinguished Flying Crosses and two Distinguished Flying Medals!

Such a crew was typical of those who survived in Bomber Command. To survive, brilliant flying ability was far less important than an immense capacity for taking pains to ensure that every crew member was on top of his job, and an absolutely rigid discipline in the air. No good bomber captain tolerated any unnecessary chatter on the intercom; it was reserved purely for essential crew communication. This crew referred to each other in the air as, skipper, navigator, engineer and so on: there was no use of first names in the air in a good crew. When one of the gunner's voices was heard on the intercom with the shout, 'Fighter port quarter – corkscrew port – NOW'; the skipper would throw the aircraft into an almost vertical bank to port, full left rudder, literally fall sideways for almost a thousand feet, wrench the aileron controls to starboard, soar into a vicious climbing turn to the right, then opposite aileron and repeat the whole manoeuvre again. This pilot practically cartwheeled his aircraft, banking savagely onto one wingtip as he raced the upper engines and cut the lower. The bomb-aimer who flew to Berlin that night was heard to tell a friend, 'I thought he was going to pull the f*****g wings off.' This pilot and, of course, much more distinguished ones who survived, such as Mick Martin, realised that the danger of a wing breaking off was as nothing compared to that of a fighter's cannon. Some other pilots, who could probably fly their aircraft better according to the textbook, banked more cautiously for fear of causing their aircraft to break up, and died.

On the ground, this crew were a close-knit entity too, they were rarely apart; if one crew member decided to go into York on a stand-day, then the whole crew went along. On nights when ops were scrubbed too late for them to get into York or Selby, then the whole crew could be seen drinking together in the Kings Head or The Four Horseshoes. Although in the air there was an absolutely rigid discipline, on the ground they referred to each other by first names, regardless of rank. They borrowed money, kit and sometimes even items of clothing off each other. It is difficult to describe the relationship that existed between the members of a good crew to someone who has not experienced it for themselves. They were more like members of a close-knit family than seven men brought together by the exigencies of war; in fact, the relationship was even closer than that of some blood relatives! They had their arguments, of course, but there was not one member of this crew that would not willingly have given his life for the others: that statement may seem to some overemotional or too dramatic, but it is a sober statement of fact.

All crews, naturally, were not as close knit as the 'Circus', and one could usually tell when a crew was beginning to break up and fall apart; such crews almost inevitably went missing. It was tragic to squadron colleagues to see this happen. Not all crews who were lost, however, were bad or indifferent ones: every man who survived Bomber Command's war will agree that luck was vital. Even the best of crews were vulnerable to the chance hit from the box barrage of anti-aircraft fire over the target, or other defended areas. A good, careful, well-disciplined crew such as 51's 'Flying Circus' could, however, increase their chances of survival immeasurably. A good navigator was a vital ingredient in a crew's chances of surviving; a navigator who could keep on track, well tucked into the 'stream', and who adhered rigidly to the flight plan and timed his course changes meticulously gave his crew a one hundred per cent better chance of a safe return from the operation. Some crews wandered off track, and either strayed over defended areas and fell victim to anti-aircraft fire, or were picked off by night fighters lurking at the edge of the bomber stream. Another factor was that some crews could fly up to a dozen or more operations without the gunners getting a glimpse of a night fighter or without being hit by anti-aircraft fire over the target – in fact, without any real problems at all. Occasionally these crews became a little blasé: reflexes numbed, vigilance flagged...When the moment of crisis came they reacted just that fraction too slowly, and another crew was lost.

In late 1943 and onwards, many first-class crews fell victim to an unsuspected method of attack by the Luftwaffe night fighters. The bombers had a blind spot immediately below the fuselage, and the night fighter pilots had discovered that it was possible to fly directly underneath a Lancaster or Halifax in safety, because no member of the crew could see directly beneath it. The Luftwaffe fitted two 20-millimetre cannon in BF 110s to fire almost vertically upward and slightly forward. The Luftwaffe gave this new weapon the code-name 'Schrage Musik' – jazz music or, literally, slanting music.

A 'Schrage Musik' attack started with the night fighter picking up the bomber on radar. As soon as the German visually sighted the bomber he lost height, then flew forward and, finally, slowly upward until he was approximately 100 feet below the bomber. The Luftwaffe pilots usually fired into the wings of the British aircraft rather than the belly of the bomber; if they fired into the bomber's belly there was likely to be a violent explosion as the bombload detonated; this could destroy the fighter as well as the bomber. Usually one short burst of cannon shells into the bomber's wings was sufficient to start a fire in the fuel tanks which, fanned by the slipstream, soon spread along the fuselage to the bomb bay, causing the bomber to explode. This gave the night fighter time to dive clear of the burning bomber before it blew up.

The British bomber crews who fell victim to 'Schrage

Musik' probably died without knowing what had hit them. Strangely, those few crews who survived a *'Schrage Musik'* attack and returned to tell of being attacked, were, for some months, disbelieved by Intelligence officers. Often there was not much these crews could tell the debriefing officer, because they did not really know how they had been hit – the Luftwaffe's upward firing guns used little tracer. The Luftwaffe was, therefore, able to use this method of attack for many months without Bomber Command being aware of it; and many good crews fell victim to it.

Through the remainder of November and December, 1943, the Command continued with its deep penetration attacks on the distant German cities, and always at intervals returning to strike against Berlin.

Christmas arrived, and with it came the usual Christmas 'stand-down' for the crews of 51 Squadron. It was a strange thing but Bomber Command at this time of the war, the height of the mass onslaught on Germany, never operated at Christmas and, as far as this writer is aware, the Luftwaffe had not attacked Britain during a Christmas period either.

On Christmas Eve there was an all ranks dance in the airmen's dining hall. By approximately 9 pm the crew of the 'Circus', apart from the navigator, was well and truly drunk, as were the majority of other squadron crews; the one outstanding exception was Mac, the 'Circus' navigator. This excellent fellow drank very little, and was available to look after the rest of the crew when needed, which was often. When drunk the pilot and mid-upper gunner usually produced from somewhere a grossly exaggerated charm, with which they both unsuccessfully attempted to lure unsuspecting WAAFs onto the dance floor. It was as well that these girls, after one look at these two drunks, wisely decided they were already booked fully for the evening; neither crewman could dance a single step, and would have probably caused grave injury to the poor girls. The evening passed off remarkably well, all things considered. There were only a few mild bouts of fisticuffs – at one stage during the evening a sergeant air-gunner was observed wrestling absentmindedly with a Squadron Leader pilot in a pool of beer in one corner. Nothing happened, however, to cause any serious concern to anyone, and a good time was had by all.

There was an early morning carol service on Christmas morning; most crews, however, gave this a miss, deciding to have a lie in, and to shave and dress to arrive in good time for a lunchtime drink in their respective messes.

It is the tradition in the RAF for the officers and NCOs to serve the 'other ranks' with Christmas dinner and, after having taken on a sufficient quantity of liquid fuel, a motley crowd of 'waiters' descended on the 'other ranks' to serve the turkey and Christmas pudding.

It was a source of amazement to the more sober among the waiters that the 'other ranks' managed to obtain their Christmas meal at all. Cutlery and broken dishes crashed to the floor with a noise like the roar of artillery. The fumes of beer, whisky and gin were breathed all over the rows of airmen and aircraftwomen, who joined with the officers and NCOs in singing all the usual songs. Soup was spilt, plates and cups were broken and uncomplaining WAAFs were kissed with more ardour and finesse than ever Gable showed.

Eventually the diners left the dining hall, leaving the 'waiters' to the washing-up. As Christmas Day wore on things became even more blurred and confused. Christmas dinner was served in the Officers' Mess, but few aircrew were present to eat it. Many aircrew officers were in the Sergeants' Mess roistering with the non-commissioned members of their crews. By late evening few aircrew were still on their feet, most had retired from the fray. The 'Circus' were, however, among those few still left in the Sergeants' Mess, when a dreadful thing occurred. The flight engineer suddenly had what appeared to be an extremely serious illness. He fell face down on the floor and began moving convulsively. The crew decided he was either having a fit, or was seriously ill from some other mysterious cause. Suddenly he became perfectly still. It was obvious to the crew that a dreadful calamity had occurred. Mac, the only sober man among them, good-naturedly joined them in doing the decent thing; and the engineer was duly 'buried' with full military honours, beneath the mess billiard table. Having thus done the decent thing, the rest of the crew continued with the serious business of the evening, and ordered another round of drinks. Some time later low moans were heard from beneath the billiard table; it appeared that a 'miracle' had occurred, the engineer was showing signs of recovery. Mac now decided that enough was enough, and so the crew valiantly attempted to negotiate the mile walk from the Sergeants' Mess to their living quarters. The real miracle of the evening was that they ever managed to reach their rooms!

Thus passed Christmas 1943 at Snaith during the height of the Battle of Berlin.

After the Christmas stand-down, the Command resumed its heavy attacks against the enemy; Berlin was still the prime target. 51 Squadron continued to play its part in these attacks: familiar faces, once again, disappeared from the messes to be replaced by new crews, who themselves were not members of the messes for long.

On 14 January, 1944, another squadron was born at Snaith when No.578 Squadron was formed from 51's 'C' Flight. At this time 51 had received some news which was greeted with enthusiasm by the crews; the squadron was to re-equip with the new Halifax Mark Three aircraft. This aircraft, with its Bristol Hercules radial engines, squared off tail fins and much cleaner lines, was a great improvement on the Mark Two the squadron had been operating. To the crews, at this time, any improvement in their equipment was welcome; anything which promised a reduction in the losses the squadron was suffering was hailed with great joy by the crews. In the event the crews discovered the Mark Three to be a superb aircraft: they were now able to operate on equal terms with the Lancasters at 19,000 to 20,000 feet, instead of struggling to reach 15,000 to 16,000 feet. The squadron's losses did not decrease, far from it; as the winter campaign wore on losses in the Command generally increased, but, at least, the crews had a fine aircraft in which they had a great deal of faith, and this did much for their confidence.

No.578 Squadron did not have to wait long to be blooded; equipped with Mark Three aircraft, carrying the unit code letters 'LK', it despatched five aircraft, one borrowed complete with crew from 51, to Berlin on the night of 20/21st of January. Early in February 578 moved to the nearby airfield of Burn, which Group Captain Tom Sawyer had been preparing for their arrival. Wing Commander Wilkerson went with the squadron as its commander. The crews of 51 were sorry to lose Wilkerson, he had been liked and respected by everyone on 51. Among the crews who moved with 578 to Burn were Flight Lieutenant M. McCreanor, who was promoted to Squadron Leader to take over a flight in the new squadron, and 'Joe' Barton, who later was to win the VC.

The new squadron commander of 51 arrived shortly afterwards. This officer was a career RAF officer, who had spent the previous war years in staff posts and Training Command. The crews may possibly have done this officer an injustice; but there was certainly not the same sympathy and feeling between the new commander and the crews that had existed during Wilkerson's time. Shortly after his arrival the new commander lectured the crews on their general appearance and behaviour; this did not go down at all well with the squadron's 'old lags', who also made various unfavourable comments on the fact that the new commander's name did not appear on the battle orders with quite the same frequency as Wing Commander Wilkerson's had done. Let no-one think that in commenting on this, the courage of the new commander is in any way being impugned; squadron commanders were required, in fact expected, to fly only once or twice a month and many commanders complied with this instruction. Others, of whom Wilkerson was just one example, far exceeded the statutory number of operations required of them. Experienced aircrews were also, it must be explained, inclined to cast a cynical eye at the actual targets their squadron commanders chose to fly against. Anyway, for whatever reason, there was not the close rapport between the new squadron commander and the crews that had existed previously.

During January and February 1944, the Command's difficulties were increasing; Berlin itself was a very difficult target to attempt to conceal from the enemy defenders. No matter what ploys the Command used, for the last hundred miles or so of the route it was clear that the bombers could be going nowhere else and, again and again, night fighters broke into the stream on the final approach to Berlin.

That winter, however, it was over the target itself that the crews found tremendous difficulties. Time and time again, the crews fought their way to the target to find it covered by impenetrable cloud. The targets the Command was attacking were far beyond OBOE range. Berlin, itself, gave no clearly defined H2S image: the difficulties of target-marking were enormous. No.8 (PFF) Group evolved what became known as the Berlin Method of marking. This meant that the Pathfinder Force dropped a constant, sustained concentration of both ground Target Indicators and Sky Markers throughout the twenty-five minutes or less of the attack. Main force crews were briefed to aim at the ground markers where they could see them; if the ground markers were not visible the bomb-aimers were instructed to bomb on the sky markers. Few crews ever glimpsed the ground through the thick cloud that winter.

The Command's losses mounted alarmingly; in January 6·1 per cent of aircraft despatched against Berlin were lost. Against Leipzig on 19 February seventy-eight aircraft were lost – 9·5 per cent of the total despatched. On 24 March, a night when unpredicted fierce winds blew most of the 'stream' off track and into heavily defended anti-aircraft belts, the Command lost seventy-three aircraft from those despatched against Berlin – 9·1 per cent.

There were nights when the night fighters and anti-aircraft gunners failed to score much success; on 1 March, 557 aircraft attacked Stuttgart for the loss of four bombers and, on 26 March the Command sent 705 aircraft against Essen and lost only nine. The Essen attack was particularly successful; Essen was within OBOE range and the marking had been extremely accurate, as indeed was the main force bombing. Contemporary German records list forty-eight factories and an impressive list of other establishments badly damaged, although the target had been completely covered by cloud.

On the night of 6 March, the crews of 51 Squadron found at briefing that they were to have a change from the deep penetration attacks they had become accustomed to. The target was the railway marshalling yards at Trappes in France. The crews were very carefully briefed on this target, and were instructed in no uncertain terms that they were to make every effort possible to ensure accurate bombing. They were told that the Command wanted the minimum loss of life among French civilians; the bombing height was to be below 8,000 feet, but crews were instructed, if necessary, to descend even lower to ensure accuracy.

The marking was to be by ground Target Indicators dropped by OBOE Mosquitoes of No.8 (PFF) Group, and the main force was to be the Halifaxes of No.4 Group. The Pathfinder Force did an excellent marking job and 4 Group's bomb-aiming was of impeccable accuracy. Many Halifax crews bombed from as low as 4,000 feet to make sure of hitting the railway yards and not the surrounding residential areas. One 51 Squadron bomb-aimer called a 'dummy run' at a height of below 4,000 feet and instructed his pilot to go round again for a second bombing run. During the left-hand circuit of the target to commence the second run the pilot asked what had gone wrong the first time. The bomb-aimer's reply shook him, 'I wasn't happy about the accuracy of the marker I was sighting on. I want to wait for another to go down'. On the second run the bombs were accurately placed on the marshalling yards. This despite quite lively opposition over the target! Such was the accuracy of 8 Group's marking and 4 Group's bombing that the yards were devastated and out of action for several weeks.

The crews that bombed Trappes did not know it at the time but they were taking part in an experimental attack that was to have an important effect on future attacks by Bomber Command.

The morning of 30 March 1944 was a dull, windy and drizzly one. Low cloud hung over the airfield at Snaith and the general opinion was that there would, in all probability, be no operational flying that night. Unknown to the 51 Squadron crews, however, shortly after 09·00 their Commander in Chief had made his decision; there would be a maximum effort attack that night and the target was Nuremberg.

Around 11·00 hrs the battle order, i.e. the list of crews flying that night, was placed on the notice-board in the crew room. The news was greeted with some slight dismay, especially among those who had been eyeing the weather with thoughts of a day in York in mind; 'ops' were scheduled, however, and there was nothing the crews could do except to carry on their normal routine. The aircraft were taken up for the customary air test, and the crews went to lunch. It was not long before the crews learned that the operation was to be another deep penetration effort; the news soon got round the station, the amount of fuel being loaded into the aircraft and consequent reduction of bombload always gave the crews a clear indication of the length of the flight they would be undertaking. The strange pre-operation atmosphere of suspense and anticipation had now settled over Snaith.

During the afternoon, whilst waiting for briefing, the crews noticed the increasing wind and the gathering clouds; many among them held the opinion that the operation would be 'scrubbed'; one or two, in fact, suggested going to the Four Horseshoes for a drink when the cancellation came through. The afternoon wore on and, in the early evening, the crews' pre-operational meal of eggs and bacon was served. At around this time a small group of civilians, who had arrived earlier in the day, were noticed by one aircrew man who asked what they were doing in the mess. He discovered they were a group of press correspondents and photographers who were to cover the activities of the squadron that night for their newspapers. After the 'ops' meal the navigators were called to their own pre-briefing; this was to enable them to prepare their charts and flight plan, a task which usually took about two hours.

Many of the remaining crew members were still of the opinion that the operation would be cancelled before the rest of the crews were summoned to main briefing; this was not to be, however, and the squadron crews assembled in the long hut used for briefing. For some of the crews it would be their first operation; the nervous strain showed on these men's faces. The more experienced crews assembled quietly and took their places at the wooden benches. The briefing was conducted by Squadron Leader Peter Hill DFC, a popular flight commander, and one of the most experienced pilots on 51. His opening words, 'Gentlemen, tonight's target is Nuremberg,' were greeted almost in silence. The crews were too intent on the large map above his head; this map showed the route to the target and the return to base, outlined in thin red ribbon pinned to the large wall map.

The route puzzled some of the more experienced crews: from Snaith the aircraft would first set course to Cottesmore, from there their course was to a dead reckoning position of 51° 50N, 2° 30E – off the Naze – the rendezvous point for the bomber stream over the North Sea; the stream would there change course south-easterly for a position 50° 30N, 4° 36E, Charleroi in Belgium; the force would then turn east and fly in a direct long leg to a point 50° 32N, 10° 36E, near Fulda, where it would make a south-easterly turn for the bombing run to Nuremberg. After bombing, the aircraft would fly due south from Nuremberg to 49° N, 11° 5E and then alter course to a point south of Stuttgart. There the bombers would alter course to a point 50° 01N, 10° E and eventually return across the English coast near Selsey Bill

It was the leg between Charleroi and Fulda that puzzled

some of the more experienced pilots and navigators on the squadron. They were used to routes that incorporated several changes of course and 'dog-legs', but this was a direct leg of some 270 miles. The crews were not aware that this route had been the source of disagreement earlier in the day; Don Bennett, the Pathfinder Force Commander, had strongly voiced his objections to the direct leg between Charleroi and Fulda and had suggested an alternative course incorporating diversionary 'dog-legs'. He had been overruled by a majority of the other Group commanders; apparently the only man to support Bennett had been 4 Group's commander, Air Vice-Marshal Carr. As far as the crews of 51 Squadron were concerned, the route shown on the wall map was the planned route and they had to fly it.

Peter Hill introduced a moment of humour into the briefing when he told the crews that, 'The Americans had been out during the day and had shot down every goddam fighter in the area'. This was a joking reference to the slightly exaggerated claims the press were currently publishing about 8th Air Force victories over Germany. Peter Hill was to fly to Nuremberg and not return; it is believed he was shot down by anti-aircraft fire near Stuttgart. There were no survivors from his crew.

Various diversionary ploys had been laid on to assist the main effort; those squadrons that had not yet completed re-equipment with the Halifax Mark Three were to despatch fifty of their Mark Twos across the North Sea, dropping large quantities of window. These aircraft would simulate an attack on Northern Germany but, before crossing the enemy coast, were to drop mines in the Heligoland Bight and return home. This diversion was timed to approach the German coast at exactly the same time as the main force was approaching the Belgian coast. It was hoped by the staff at High Wycombe that this would fox the German defenders and split the night fighter force. Bennett had laid on three 'spoof' attacks by his Mosquitoes, on Aachen, Cologne and Kassel. Each of these attacks by Bennett's aircraft would drop window and large numbers of target indicators together with 4,000 lb bombs to simulate the opening of a large scale attack. The Aachen and Cologne 'spoofs' were intended to keep the night fighters in the Ruhr area, whilst the Kassel attack was intended to lure the night fighters to the north-east away from the bomber stream.

100 Group were also mounting a maximum effort with their 'Serrate' night fighter Mosquitoes in support of the bombers, and intruder night fighters would attack known German night fighter airfields; there were some unusual aircraft among the intruders. The 8th Air Force had recently sent two Lightnings and two Mustangs on detachment to RAF Station Little Snoring, and these were to operate with 100 Group's aircraft.

Briefing over, 51's crews went to their aircraft; the squadron commenced take-off at approximately 22·00 hrs. All went well, and the operation got off to a good start. The squadron despatched seventeen aircraft that night, to the usual accompaniment of waves and cheers from their well-wishers at the end of the runway. As the bombers set course over Snaith the crews were unaware that they were heading for the greatest and most savage air battle the world has known.

Bomber Command despatched a total of 795 Lancasters and Halifax Mark Three aircraft against Nuremberg; including 110 Pathfinder Force aircraft. The German night fighter controllers picked up the assembly of this huge force early, and were not misled by the diversionary mine-laying force heading toward the Heligoland Bight. The German defenders kept a tight grip on the main effort's route and, as the British force approached the Belgian coast, General Schmidt, the German night fighter commander, ordered his aircraft into the air. The fighters were ordered to orbit a beacon code-named Ida, south-east of Cologne; those Luftwaffe fighters that could not reach Ida were ordered to orbit a second beacon, Otto, just north of Frankfurt.

The British bomber crews had been told at briefing that there would be high cloud along their route which would afford them concealment against the night fighters. As the bomber crews flew across Belgium and into German airspace they realised that the weather forecast was wrong; the skies were clear and they were fully exposed to the light of a half moon! They were also leaving dense condensation trails in their wake, although flying well below the height at which these tell-tale trails were usually produced. Another unforeseen hazard was that, due to unexpected high winds, the stream had already begun to lose concentration and to spread over a broad belt to the north of track. It was in this form that the stream flew into German airspace. 51's 'Flying Circus' were operating that night and, due to the excellent standard of Mac, their navigator, had already realised that they were ahead of their allotted place in the stream and slightly north of track. Accordingly they commenced a dog-leg to regain their place in the stream and to get back on track. No crew liked doing this, but it was obviously necessary, so the pilot commenced the dogleg. This consisted of altering course 60 degrees to port for one minute and swinging 120 degrees back, flying two sides of an equilateral triangle. It was whilst flying this dog-leg that the crew were fired on for the only time that night, by another British bomber, below and slightly ahead of them. A trigger-happy gunner loosed off a stream of fire from his rear turret which fortunately was inaccurate and passed harmlessly above their port wing!

Shortly after this incident the bomber stream ran into the massed German fighters orbiting Ida and a running air battle developed which lasted all the way to the target; a distance of some 250 miles from Aachen eastwards, past the second beacon, Otto, and on southward to Nuremberg, with ever-increasing numbers of night fighters attacking as the enemy correctly divined the target. The British aircraft were easy prey, exposed in the moonlight, and the route was strewn with the burning wrecks of the bombers. Probably more than 50 British aircraft were shot down on the leg between Charleroi and Fulda.

On reaching the target the crews found their troubles

were by no means over. Along the route the skies had been clear, over the target there was thick cloud; in addition the unexpectedly high winds blew both the Pathfinders and the main force eastward on the southerly leg into Nuremberg. The Pathfinders were forced to use sky markers, due to the thick cloud, and as soon as the markers' parachutes opened, the high winds blew these even further to the east of the city. The bombing was scattered and inaccurate. Some crews failed to reach Nuremberg at all, and a number of bombs were dropped on Schweinfurt by mistake. German night fighters were still attacking over the target itself, and several bombers were shot down in the vicinity of Nuremberg.

By the time the British aircraft turned on the homeward leg south of Stuttgart they were widely dispersed. The mass onslaught by the night fighters had now ceased, the fighters had to land to refuel and re-arm. It is believed that at least fourteen British aircraft fell victim to anti-aircraft fire somewhere along this part of the route; among them were Peter Hill and his crew.

Even for the crews that reached Britain after this nightmare over Germany, there was still trouble. Fog and scattered sleet and snow caused large numbers of aircraft to be diverted from their home bases; aircraft were landing anywhere they could all over Eastern England. From the seventeen bombers despatched from Snaith, only three landed back at base, among them the 'Circus'.

This was the worst night Bomber Command experienced in the whole of the Second World War. Of the 795 aircraft despatched against Nuremberg, 95 failed to return; 10 crashed in England; a further 70 suffered severe battle damage – one was written off due to this. From all operations that night, including diversionary attacks, the total losses were 108 aircraft.

51 Squadron itself suffered the highest percentage losses in the Command. The squadron had despatched seventeen Halifax aircraft to Nuremberg; five failed to return and one, piloted by Pilot Officer J. Brooks who had flown 19

operations with the squadron, crashed at Stokenchurch in Oxfordshire on its return with the loss of the entire crew. These six aircraft represented a loss rate of 35 per cent. Of the 119 men who had taken off to attack Nuremberg, 35 were dead and 7 were prisoners of the Germans. There was also one man wounded in one of the aircraft that returned safely.

578 Squadron at Burn had lost one aircraft missing, but two of the squadron's aircraft were wrecked in crashes in England; both these aircraft were flown by former 51 crews. S/Ldr. McCreanor was killed trying to land his badly damaged aircraft at the OTU airfield at Silverstone; there was only one survivor from this crash. Pilot Officer Barton was killed in a crash at Ryhope in County Durham.

The Nuremberg operation was Cyril Barton's 18th; he had already earned a reputation for courage and determination on his previous raids. Barton's aircraft had been badly hit on the route to the target, and had sustained severe damage. The turrets were out of action, radio and intercom unserviceable, one engine out of action and two fuel tanks leaking. With the intercom out of action Barton's gunners were using the emergency button-controlled light system to communicate evasive action to him; the three men in the nose of the bomber misinterpreted these signals as an order to abandon aircraft and baled out. Barton was now without his navigator, bomb-aimer and wireless operator, and was flying a badly crippled aircraft. No-one in Bomber Command would have blamed him if he had given up, and either baled out with the rest of the crew, or at least jettisoned his bombload and turned for home. Instead, he pressed on to the target and dropped his bombs on the sky markers over Nuremberg, or what he took to be Nuremberg. He had now the long return flight, with no navigator or wireless operator. His exact route to England will never be known, but it was an epic of courage and determination. He calculated rough courses himself and, according to his surviving crew members, they encountered no further trouble over enemy territory. The sea crossing seemed to go on and on, and all removable equipment was jettisoned into the sea. Barton was probably intending to cross the English coast somewhere in East Anglia but it appears the bomber actually flew up the east coast of England, but just out of sight of land. He eventually made landfall at Ryhope, a mining town on the Durham coast. As he flew over this place his fuel supply finally gave out; ordering the three remaining members of his crew to the crash position by the main spar of the Halifax Barton, with hardly any control of the aircraft, attempted a crash landing. Unfortunately, in the path of the Halifax were some miners' cottages and, even in his extreme peril, Barton attempted to avoid these, lifting the nose of the aircraft to clear them. This robbed the aircraft of all flying speed and it crashed into the yard of the local coal-mine. The three men in the crash position survived, but Cyril Barton was killed.

In June 1944 it was announced that Cyril Barton had been awarded a posthumous Victoria Cross. Cyril, or 'Joe' as he was known to many of the aircrew of 51, was a quiet, unassuming, devoutly-Christian young man. Those surviving aircrew of 578 and 51 Squadrons who knew him consider themselves privileged.

Much has been written since the war years about the Nuremberg operation, and it has been the subject of much controversy not only among historians but, also, among Bomber Command aircrew. In the Official History, Webster and Frankland comment, 'The operation suffered the ill consequences of unusually bad luck and uncharacteristically bad and unimaginative planning'. This comment itself has been the subject of much controversy.

The late Sir Robert Saundby, Deputy Commander in Chief Bomber Command, has been quoted, 'The weather conditions were so bad that the timing went completely wrong. It...was one of the few occasions when everything went wrong...We were not such fools as the Official History suggests, the straight flight plan seemed the lesser of two evils'.

Sir Ralph Cochrane, the brilliantly imaginative commander of No.5 Group, agreed with Saundby. Before he died, Cochrane was quoted as saying, 'It is hard to see that any other route would necessarily have been better.... The criticism of the long straight run in is open to question, for it will be noted that the German fighters had no difficulty in following the force when it turned south-east, near Fulda'. To the end of his life Sir Ralph dissented strongly with the Official Historian's comment on 'bad planning'.

Air Vice-Marshal Donald Bennett, the Pathfinder Force Commander, commented that the sentence in the Official History concerning bad planning is about the only thing in the Official History with which he agrees!

There is no doubt that the long leg from Charleroi to Fulda went against all the previously carefully planned tactical diversions and feints which were always a part of every route planned by Don Bennett and his staff at No.8 (PFF) Group HQ: whether these diversions would have made much difference that night is, however, open to question. The Luftwaffe controllers, in a way, took a gamble by ordering all their night fighters into the air early; they were aided by the clear weather conditions along the route and, once the fighters had made contact with the stream, it is doubtful whether any amount of tactical trickery would have shaken them off. Sir Arthur Harris was probably more realistic than anyone else when he stated that he was surprised there were not more nights similar to Nuremberg during the long campaign against Germany.

The American writer Morrison called the Nuremberg raid, 'One of the most badly planned and executed attacks flown by Bomber Command'. A statement of that stupidity is not worth commenting on!

At Snaith on the morning of 31 March, there was a certain amount of shock at the scale of losses: but, contrary to what some writers have claimed, there was very little gloom and despondency; not at Snaith anyway and, as far as this writer is aware, not in the Command generally. Bomber Command aircrews, by and large, were a fairly resilient bunch of young men. They were shocked by the loss of their friends and comrades; there was, however, nothing they could do about it. The war still had to be fought, and they were the ones who had to fight the air war. The Command did not operate that night, indeed there were few operations for some days; it was now well into the moon period and crews that were due for leave went off to enjoy the six days' rest. The routine at Snaith carried on as usual, except that there were more telegrams to be sent to relatives of the missing men, and more rooms for the men of the 'Committee of Adjustment' to clear of personal belongings. Within a few hours, eager new crews began arriving from the Heavy Conversion Units to take the place of the men who had been lost. The older crews, those that were not due for leave, either journeyed into York or spent an even wilder evening than usual at the Kings Head or Four Horseshoes.

At this time the crews did not know it, but the Battle of Berlin was over: Nuremberg was the last operation of the battle.

Of the 51 Squadron crews that fought through the Battle of Berlin few survived. It had been a long, bitter winter for the aircrews of Bomber Command: soon they would embark upon an entirely different type of campaign.

CHAPTER THIRTEEN

During the winter of 1943/4, there was a growing body of opinion amongst staff officers at Air Ministry that the Commander in Chief of Bomber Command was not paying sufficient attention to some targets listed by the Ministry of Economic Warfare as being vital to Germany's war production. Principal among these were the ball-bearing plants at Erkner, Steyr, Cannstatt and, the main bone of contention, the ball-bearing factories at Schweinfurt. Harris was never very impressed with the opinion of the experts at the Ministry of Economic Warfare; maybe the report of the Lloyd committee on oil in the early days of the bombing war had something to do with Harris's scathing denunciation of these experts as 'Panacea Mongers'.

As early as July 1943, Group Captain Bufton, the Director of Bomber Operations at Air Ministry, had been persuaded by the Ministry of Economic Warfare that the destruction of Schweinfurt would cripple Germany and bring the enemy to his knees: Bufton pressed for attacks by the 8th Air Force and Bomber Command. Spaatz and Eaker agreed with Bufton and were eager to attack Schweinfurt. Sir Arthur Harris, however, was rather less sanguine about the success of such an attack.

Schweinfurt was a very small target, and extremely difficult to find and mark accurately at night. If the 8th Air Force were prepared to attack in daylight then, as far as Harris was concerned, that was a decision for their commanders. In any case, Harris did not believe the destruction of Schweinfurt and its ball-bearing plants would prove to be the crippling blow to Germany that the economic experts claimed. The 8th Air Force attacked Schweinfurt in August and October 1943, and it was, in fact, the Luftwaffe that then struck an almost crippling blow against the Americans.

In November, the experts at the Ministry of Economic Warfare again pressed for attacks against Schweinfurt; again Harris resisted pressure from Air Ministry to attack. There was lengthy correspondence between Harris and Air Ministry over this matter; on 20 December Harris wrote to Air Ministry clearly stating his reasons for objecting:

'The town is in the very centre – by any angle of approach – of the most heavily defended part of Germany. It is extremely small and difficult to find. It is heavily defended, including smoke-screens. In these circumstances it might need up to six or seven full-scale attacks before a satisfactory result was secured on the town as a whole. Even then the chances of individual factories being written off are dubious.'

On 14 January, 1944, the Air Ministry sent Harris a directive which ordered him to attack Schweinfurt 'in force on the first opportunity when weather and other conditions allow'.

On the afternoon of 24th February, the 8th Air Force attacked the town in daylight; this time, thanks to the long-range Mustang fighter escort, losing eleven aircraft compared with the crippling losses of August and October 1943.

The same night, in good weather conditions, Bomber Command despatched a force of 734 aircraft carrying a bombload of some 2,260 tons, to follow up the American attack. Bomber Command's attack was a failure; and 33 aircraft were lost for little result. Harris had been right, Schweinfurt was not an easy target for his force to locate, mark and bomb at night.

Sir Arthur Harris was correct on another score. During his exchanges with Air Ministry, Harris said he did not accept the claims made by the economic experts and pointed out in a letter dated 20 December 1943:

'The actual percentage of Germany's ball-bearing supply manufactured in Schweinfurt has always been exaggerated and has been progressively reduced, even by the authors. At this stage of the war I am confident that the Germans have long ago made every possible effort to disperse so vital a production.'

Indeed the Germans had; after the second American attack in October 1943, Albert Speer, Reichminister for Armaments, had put into effect a speedy dispersal of the ball-bearing production.

Speer has gone on record as being of the opinion that the frequency of attack against Schweinfurt, and also Germany's other main ball-bearing production centres, would have had to be three or four times every two weeks, simultaneously against all plants, to bring production to a standstill. This, before he had put in hand the dispersal of the industry. This would have been impossible for either the 8th Air Force or Bomber Command; the 8th would have suffered heavy loss attempting this, and Bomber Command could never have achieved this task at night. The ballbearing targets were out of range for Bomber Command for much of the year, because of the short nights. What the experts at the Ministry of Economic Warfare appeared to fail to understand was that such a wasted effort by Bomber Command would have spared the rest of Germany, and given the enemy the space he desperately needed to regain ascendancy in the air, and to rehabilitate the badly-hit industrial centres and cities.

Over the question of the ball-bearing 'panacea' it would appear that Sir Arthur Harris's 'inexpert guess', as some critics have contemptuously referred to his opinion, was far more accurate than the opinion held by the experts at the Ministry of Economic Warfare.

During the early months of 1944 there was growing concern at Air Ministry over the mounting losses of Bomber Command. Since the war some of Sir Arthur Harris's critics have suggested that Portal should have sacked Harris at the end of February or early March; they have suggested that Harris was virtually defying Portal in continuing the long-range deep-penetration saturation attacks on distant German cities. Correspondence between Harris and Portal does not suggest that this interpretation is correct. Portal, in fact, was one of the people who was, in the autumn and early winter of 1943, pressing Harris to attack Berlin. Another figure of authority who was constantly urging heavy attacks on the German capital, and other major cities, was Prime Minister Churchill.

Harris's critics have attempted to portray him as some kind of blind, obstinate, callous commander, who cared little, if at all, about the heavy casualties his men were suffering. Nothing could be further from the truth. The reason Harris was reluctant to attempt any precision attacks over Germany itself, was precisely because he refused to, as he saw it, throw his crews' lives away needlessly on targets on which they would be unable to achieve satisfactory results.

Harris did not wreck Berlin 'from end to end' as he had prophesied, and he lost almost three times as many aircraft as he forecast. Tremendous devastation was done to the German capital, however, and also to the other major cities the Command had attacked. If Portal had been so much in disagreement with what Harris was setting out to achieve over Germany then all he had to do was to issue a direct order to Harris. Harris was never afraid of putting his own opinions forward to either Portal or the Air Staff; if he had not been such a forthright character he would not have been the great commander he was, but whenever given a direct order he always carried it out, with good grace, and to the best of his considerable ability.

Marshal of the Royal Air Force Sir Dermot Boyle, who served as a Wing Commander on the Chiefs of Staff Secretariat, has been quoted as saying (by Portal's biographer, Denis Richards) 'If Portal had thought that Harris was not doing well for the country, Harris would have been out in five minutes'.

In the event Harris and Bomber Command did not achieve the great victory in the Battle of Berlin that Harris hoped for. In the words of Sir Ralph Cochrane, 'Berlin was just too tough a nut'. In the Official History, Webster and Frankland say, 'It was a defeat'. In making this claim, however, the

Official Historians appear to ignore the words of Albert Speer, who wrote in his secret diary in Spandau prison:

'The real importance of the air war consisted in the fact that it opened a second front long before the invasion of Europe. That front was the skies over Germany. Defence against air attack required the production of thousands of anti-aircraft guns, the stockpiling of tremendous quantities of ammunition all over the country, and holding in readiness hundreds of thousands of soldiers ... As far as I can judge from the accounts I have read, no-one has yet seen that this was the greatest lost battle on the German side.'

To the end of his life Sir Arthur Harris would argue that had he been given the resources he sought, and permitted to continue the assault on Germany into the summer of 1944, the war would have been ended months sooner. His critics claim that, had this happened, Bomber Command would have faced ultimate defeat. Which view would have proved correct will never be known: from 14 April 1944, Bomber Command and the 8th Air Force were placed under the direction of the Supreme Allied Commander, General Eisenhower, to carry out operations in direct support of the Allied invasion of Europe. From that date, until further notice, the Allied heavy bomber forces would carry out strategic operations only with the consent of the Supreme Commander.

An example of Harris bowing to orders from higher authority was the Transportation Plan. This plan, which was devised by Professor Solly Zuckerman, was a comprehensive strategy for the destruction of every key rail-link in Northern France. The Allied planners of the invasion had concluded that the greatest threat would come in the 'build up' period after the landings; unless the enemy could be drastically impeded the planners were afraid the Germans would be able to concentrate divisions around the bridge-head more quickly than the Allies would be able to reinforce it. Eisenhower and his deputy, Air Chief Marshal Tedder, were convinced the Transportation Plan was the best means of wrecking the enemy communications with Normandy, and also the most effective use of the heavy bomber force before the invasion. Portal was also convinced the plan would work; Harris and the American General Spaatz, however, did not agree. Harris was not convinced his crews could attack such small targets without large loss of life to French civilians. Churchill was also opposed to the plan; he was appalled by estimates that up to 40,000 French civilians could be killed.

Eisenhower persisted, however, in pressing for the plan to be adopted and eventually Churchill agreed. Harris still opposed the plan but eventually, given a direct order from Portal he, as always, obeyed his superior officer. The accuracy of the attack on Trappes surprised Harris; he followed Trappes with further experimental attacks against such rail centres as Aulnoye, Le Mans, Coutrai, Laon and Amiens/Lougeau. The attacks were a triumph for the aircrews of Bomber Command. Harris was, in fact, surprised by the virtuosity of his own crews! They achieved astounding accuracy on these yards, and the casualties to the French were far, far lower than had been estimated. The interdiction of enemy communications behind the battle front in Normandy is now part of history. The crews of Bomber Command bore the major burden of the Transportation Plan attacks. In March, 1944, 70 per cent of all Bomber Command's bombs fell on German targets; in April less than fifty per cent, in May less than a quarter. In June practically the entire weight of Bomber Command's effort was directed against targets in Northern France.

The 8th Air Force played little part in the Transportation Plan attacks; it was the aircrews of Bomber Command who were mainly responsible for destroying the enemy links with the Normandy battleground. The crews were actually achieving greater accuracy by night than the 8th Air Force by day. In all the pre-invasion bombing a total of 12,000 French and Belgians were killed. Dreadful as these casualties were, they were far less than the 40,000 the plan's authors had originally estimated.

In early 1944, whilst the main force were fighting the Battle of Berlin, some very interesting developments had been taking place in No.5 Group. No. 617 Squadron, now based at Woodhall Spa, was under the command of Wing Commander G. L. Cheshire, a distinguished and much decorated former No.4 Group pilot. Leonard Cheshire had, actually, been promoted to Group Captain at the age of 25 and had voluntarily dropped his rank to take over 617.

617 had been given the task of attacking some concrete platforms in Northern France which the Intelligence people had identified as launching platforms for the German V-weapons. During these attacks Cheshire, together with S/Ldr H.B. (Mick) Martin, had tried low-level marking of the target in Lancasters. They had placed their ideas before Air Vice-Marshal Cochrane who, always receptive to ideas to improve bombing accuracy, had encouraged them in their efforts. On 8 February 1944, Cheshire and Martin marked the Gnome Rhone engine factory from a height of 200 feet. The remaining Lancasters of 617 then proceeded to demolish the factory with extraordinary accuracy.

Cochrane then suggested that they attack the Antheor Viaduct on the Italian coast. The viaduct was only the width of its railway tracks broad. Fifteen thousand tons of supplies for the German forces at Anzio crossed it daily. To destroy it 617 had to place a 12,000 lb. bomb within ten yards.

Despite tremendously determined efforts by both Cheshire and Martin this attack was not successful; the defences around the viaduct were formidable and both pilots found themselves facing an almost impenetrable barrage of fire. Martin's aircraft was badly hit just as he was about to release his markers. His bomb-aimer Bob Hay was killed, and his engineer badly injured. Apart from the damaged nose of the aircraft, Martin had two engines badly damaged, his bomb doors were stuck in the down position, the air pressure for his brake controls had gone, and he still had most of his bombload aboard. It was obvious he would not be able to reach England; he headed for the American landing strip at Elmas in Sardinia. The crew managed to jettison most of the bombload manually over the sea, and Martin executed a skilful landing in Sardinia. Bob Hay was interred there, and after repairs locally and at Blida, North Africa, Martin flew his Lancaster back to England. Cochrane decided that this exceptionally gifted and courageous pilot had done enough, and he was posted to a staff post at HQ No.100 Group. It was not long before Martin was battling with authority to get back to operational flying and, within a very short time, he was back flying Mosquitoes on intruder sorties over enemy territory. After Martin had headed out to sea from the Antheor Viaduct Cheshire finally succeeded in placing his markers near the viaduct; although 617's bomb-aimers determinedly tried to hit the viaduct the attack failed, by a matter of feet!

Cheshire and Cochrane were both convinced, however, that an aircraft different to a Lancaster was needed for the technique to be successful. Cochrane agreed to suggest to Harris that the squadron be provided with some Mosquito aircraft. In the meantime the squadron continued with its attacks on targets in France, still with Cheshire marking at low level in his Lancaster. All targets were destroyed with absolute precision.

When Cochrane approached Harris he found his commander in a receptive mood; Harris agreed to let 617 have their Mosquitoes; in fact he went much further; he arranged for the transfer of No.627 Squadron of Mosquitoes together with 83 and 97 Lancaster squadrons from No.8 (PFF) Group to No.5 Group. 627 to carry out low-level marking, and the Lancaster squadrons to be the illuminators for the Mosquitoes.

Don Bennett was outraged at this and fought strenuously to retain his squadrons; but despite all his efforts he lost the battle and his squadrons came under Cochrane's command, although No.8 (PFF) Group would be responsible for providing crews, and for training new crews, for the squadrons. Bennett rang Sir Robert Saundby at High Wycombe and, in typically outspoken manner, asked where his replacement aircraft and crews were to come from when those detached to 5 Group had been shot down!

There is no doubt that there was some personal antipathy between Don Bennett and Cochrane; Cochrane is understood to have been one of the senior officers who was against Bennett being appointed to command of the Pathfinders. They were both outstandingly competent group commanders and, despite their personal antipathy, there is no evidence that their antagonism ever descended to pettiness. Certainly, neither man allowed it to affect his conduct of the war against the common enemy.

By transferring the three squadrons to No.5 Group, and encouraging Cochrane in his efforts in low level marking, Sir Arthur Harris got the best out of both these exceptionally gifted group commanders. Once again, however, Harris found himself being criticised by some of the staff at Air Ministry.

An angry Harris wrote to Portal:

'...ideas on Pathfinders, as on some other matters, have always been and still are rammed down our throats whether we liked them or not, and that on occasions more weight is given to opinions of a junior officer two years out of Command than to the considered opinions of the Commanders on the spot who are responsible for the outcome of events.'

In a way, Cochrane was lucky with his timing of the low-level marking. It would have been impracticable, even suicidal, to attempt it over the targets attacked during the Battle of Berlin period; the timing was exactly right for the future conduct of 5 Group's operations, however, and the Group achieved outstanding success with it for the remainder of the war.

Together with Leonard Cheshire, Mick Martin was the pilot mainly responsible for the low-level marking technique.

Cheshire himself has described Martin as, 'The greatest operational bomber pilot the RAF has ever produced'. Few Bomber Command men would argue with that description.

On 24 April, Cheshire and three other 617 pilots, Shannon, Kearns and Fawkes, carried out an accurate low level marking exercise on Munich for a main force of 5 Group's Lancasters. Munich was very accurately, and heavily, bombed for the first time during the war. Previous attempts had been made on this target, but none had been a success.

Leonard Cheshire was awarded a Victoria Cross for his outstanding leadership of 617 Squadron, for his low-level attack on Munich, and for his long and courageous record of operational flying over enemy territory.

As D-Day for the great invasion of Northern Europe approached, the Command continued its attacks on the rail centres of Northern France, together with attacks on German military installations and troop concentrations, 5 Group operating more and more as a separate force using its own low level marker aircraft, whilst 8 (PFF) Group continued to provide OBOE marking for the other groups. Both methods of marking were now providing exceptional bombing accuracy from the respective main forces. The Command's efforts during the build-up to the actual landings undoubtedly saved thousands of Allied troops' lives on 6 June 1944.

On the night of the actual invasion, the Command was out in great strength, attacking gun emplacements, radar installations, road junctions, vital targets of all types. 617 Squadron took part in a brilliantly executed 'spoof' which was code-named 'taxable'. An illusion of a mass of shipping was given to enemy radar in Pas de Calais by dropping window along paths spaced two miles apart. The aircraft flew in boxes of four, flying straight tracks four miles apart and about eight miles along a GEE lattice line toward the enemy coast, then doing an accurate rate-one turn, through 180 degrees, onto a course parallel to and two miles from the inward course, and finally completing the orbit with a rate-one turn within seven minutes. One box of four aircraft patrolled on the length 30/38 miles from the coast, the second box 38/46 miles away, the first four flying at 3,000 feet, the second at 2,500, each dropping bundles of window at the rate of 36 bundles during each leg of every orbit. This appeared on radar screens as ships heading for the coast at eight knots. This was flying that demanded the utmost in precision and accuracy. The squadron was brilliantly successful, flying at 160 mph, keeping correct height by radio altimeter and timing their turns by stop-watch.

No. 218 Squadron also took part in the operation with a similar 'spoof' off Boulogne. Both squadrons performed outstandingly well and the deception was a complete success. The enemy was convinced a landing was about to take place in the Pas de Calais area.

The summer of 1944 was a hectic one for the crews of Bomber Command: the Command was now operating over France in daylight, as well as by night. Some outstanding attacks were mounted in close support of Allied troops. Over Northern France at this time large streams of bombers rarely attacked a single target in saturation attacks. Single squadrons were operating against individual targets, bombing markers placed by OBOE Mosquito aircraft. To obscure the Allies' intentions in Normandy it was necessary to attack marshalling yards, airfields, radar, wireless installations, enemy armour and troops with equal intensity from Cherbourg to Belgium. The targets required great accuracy from limited numbers of aircraft; and the Command's aircrews provided exactly the accuracy required.

In June 1944, Bomber Command despatched 15,963 sorties, as against 5,816 in June 1943. Harris, having put the whole weight of Bomber Command behind the Transportation Plan and the pre-invasion attacks, felt that his personnel were not receiving sufficient recognition for the tremendous efforts and achievements. On 1 July 1944 he wrote to the Chief of Air Staff:

'I think you should be aware of the full depth of feeling that is being aroused by the lack of adequate or even reasonable credit to the RAF in particular and the air forces as a whole, for their efforts in the invasion. I have no personal ambition that has not years ago been satisfied in full, but I for one cannot forbear a most emphatic protest against the grave injustice which is being done to my crews. There are over 10,500 aircrew in my operational squadrons. In three months we have lost over half that number. They have a right that their story should be adequately told, and it is a military necessity that it should be.'

Harris was, as usual, correct in making this point. It was not known to the British people that, in making their tremendous effort in support of the Allied armies, Bomber Command's aircrew casualties in the first weeks after D-Day were higher than those of the British Second Army in Normandy.

CHAPTER FOURTEEN

By late summer and early autumn 1944, many of the Allied leaders appeared to believe that the collapse of Germany was near at hand. The politicians seemed to think it no longer mattered what the heavy bombers attacked, as long as they were available to give tactical support to the ground troops when needed.

In July, the Chiefs of Staff forwarded a minute to Prime Minister Churchill:

'The time might well come in the not too distant future when an all-out attack by every means at our disposal on German civilian morale might be decisive...'

The importance of this minute, and the reason it is highlighted in this book, is that it proved that support for area bombing still existed in places of high authority. The fact that this minute was signed by all the Chiefs of Staff, and was accepted by the Prime Minister, proves that the concept of attacking German cities was not a unilateral decision by Air Chief Marshal Sir Arthur Harris, as so many people have been led to believe since the war. This concept was not even a unilateral air force enthusiasm.

Tedder showed great interest in the possibility of a massive attack on German civilian morale; Portal for a time seemed in favour of it. There was discussion of a possible four days and nights' assault on Berlin; it was thought this might bring about the collapse of the Nazi regime. The point of importance is that none of the Allied leaders opposed a resumption of area bombing.

Sir Arthur Harris had never lost faith in the course on which he embarked over two and a half years earlier. Before, during, and after the invasion he had wholeheartedly committed his force to support of the Allied ground forces, and the Command had played its part with overwhelming effect. As the German air defence crumbled and Bomber Command losses fell, Harris found himself with over one thousand front-line bombers available daily, a surplus of trained aircrews, and a range of techniques and devices beyond the Command's wildest dreams two years earlier. Sir Arthur Harris had to obtain the approval of the Supreme Commander before attacking any strategic target; in August Tedder and Eisenhower agreed that the Allied armies were becoming too careless in their requests for heavy bomber support, even in the most unsuitable circumstances. That month the Supreme Commander gave approval for Bomber Command to attack German cities; authority for twelve attacks was issued from Supreme Headquarters, Allied Expeditionary Forces. The biggest of these attacks was on 16 August, when 809 aircraft attacked Kiel and Stettin.

On 29 August a small force of 175 Lancasters attacked Königsberg, causing great devastation. On 11 September, 5 Group attacked the town of Darmstadt. 218 Lancasters and 14 Mosquitoes delivered an exceptionally effective attack which virtually destroyed it. To attack Darmstadt 5 Group used a new 'offset' bombing technique; this meant, in effect, that instead of bombing along a single axis, the aircraft would make their bombing runs along seven different aiming lines at varying heights. Every aircraft would vary its delay in bombing after passing the marker point by between three and twelve seconds. This meant that, instead of a single mass of destruction, the bombing would be spread evenly the entire length and breadth of the target. To ensure that the key industrial targets were destroyed after the Lancasters had bombed, seven of 627 Squadron's Mosquitoes would go in low to strike at the key factories. In all 399 tons of high explosive and 580 tons of incendiary bombs would be dropped; not a huge bombload compared with some other attacks. In the event Darmstadt suffered heavy damage, and a firestorm similar to that of Hamburg raged in the town. The attack destroyed 4,064 out of 8,401 houses; 570 shops were

also destroyed, the Rohm and Haas factory was severely
damaged, the diesel engine works very heavily damaged and
the Merck factory damaged. The prison and the post office
were about the only public buildings left standing. Over
49,000 people fled the city as refugees; it is not possible to
estimate the number of people killed in the attack, although
contemporary German records estimate 6,049 killed, 4,502
missing and 3,749 wounded. Since the war a number of
writers have tried to imply that Darmstadt was a provincial
town of no importance; that its people were somehow
possessed of some sort of unique innocence and free of the
taint of Nazism. Darmstadt's factories were as important as
any others to the Nazi war economy. The town had important
chemical factories that produced materials essential for the
Nazi war machine, not beer steins or cuckoo clocks! The
people of Darmstadt were just as prepared to support the
Nazi leadership as those of Berlin or Frankfurt, no more and
no less. What happened to Darmstadt was only the same kind
of destruction as had been meted out by the German armed
forces to so many other towns throughout Europe. Bomber
Command was undoubtedly more efficient than the
Germans, but the writers who hold their heads in horror at the
destruction of Darmstadt would do well to remember that the
tales of the horrific suffering of the Darmstadters were
nothing to the suffering of the millions of French, Dutch,
Poles, British and Russians since 1939; and could not be
compared with the sufferings of the 6,000,000 or more Jews
who died in the Nazi extermination camps.

Bomber Command was now able to administer such
blows to Germany almost at will; and would do so until the
end of the war.

In the last stages of the war, between October 1944 and
May 1945, the Allied Strategic Bomber Forces played a
dominant part in bringing about the collapse of the German
economy. Against ineffectual resistance from the Luftwaffe,
the 8th Air Force by day, and Bomber Command by night,

attacked Germany on an unprecedented scale. Bomber Command dropped a greater weight of bombs in the last quarter of 1944 than in the whole of 1943.

The bombers' destruction of Germany's oil resources was largely responsible for the breakdown of the enemy offensive in the Ardennes at the end of 1944, and probably hastened the end of the war by several weeks. The attacks on rail and water communications were strangling German industry to death by the end of 1944.

By the end of September 1944, the 8th Air Force and Bomber Command had brought German oil production almost to a standstill. The Luftwaffe pilot-training programme had practically ceased because of a shortage of aircraft fuel. The Luftwaffe was hardly able to operate its front-line aircraft for the same reason. The German armies were driven back on horse-drawn transport; diesel trucks were towing petrol-driven vehicles; tank formations were immobilised; battlefield mobility was seriously affected and fuel stockpiles were becoming exhausted.

On 14 September 1944, control of the heavy bomber forces reverted from General Eisenhower to General Spaatz and Portal. The 'Pointblank' directive was again the guiding instruction to the bomber commanders. The aim was still, 'to bring about the progressive destruction of the German military, industrial and economic systems'. Support of the armies remained a major responsibility and 'important industrial areas' were to be attacked 'when weather or tactical conditions are unsuitable for operations against specific primary objectives'.

The orders were a disappointment to Tedder, the Deputy Supreme Commander; he wanted the bombers to repeat the bombing of French rail-links against the German rail-links. The 8th Air Force did carry out a number of attacks against German railyards and communication centres, but as these attacks were all carried out bombing blind through cloud using H2X they were really area bombing attacks on German towns and cities. The term the Americans have used to describe these attacks since the war is nothing but hypocritical 'window dressing'. The American History describes these attacks as 'blind bombing of transportation centres'. Since the best circular probable error the 8th Air Force ever achieved – in early 1945 – in operations using H2X, was two miles, these attacks amounted purely and simply to area bombing. Yet still the American official historians can write:

'It is not surprising that proposals for all-out attacks on Berlin, the Ruhr or other critical areas of Germany always seemed to come from the British, who had undergone the German raids of 1940–41, and were now enduring the punishment of V1 and V2s. All proposals frankly aimed at breaking the morale of the German people met the consistent opposition of General Spaatz, who repeatedly raised the moral issues involved, and American air force headquarters in Washington strongly supported him on the ground that such operations were contrary to air force policy and national ideals.'

This is nothing but hypocritical cant! Yet since the war a belief has grown that it was Bomber Command, and Bomber Command alone, that was responsible for the area bombing of Germany. Every airman who fought over Germany knows that there was little to distinguish between the accuracy of the American or British bombing. One does not want to draw invidious comparisons; but to answer some of the accusations made against Bomber Command by certain writers, including a number of Americans, it is necessary to point out that the really accurate precision attacks of the Second World War, for example the Ruhr Dams, the sinking of the *Tirpitz,* the outstandingly accurate bombing of the French rail system and many other such feats, were carried out by the much maligned Bomber Command.

Just one example of the accuracy the Command was able to achieve was the breaching of the Dortmund Ems canal. On

23 September 1944 a breach was made in the canal at a point where the level of water was above the surrounding countryside. Five Mosquitoes of 627 Squadron were detailed to carry out the low-level marking. 125 Lancasters of 5 Group, carrying 1,000 lb. bombs, and 617 Squadron with 12,000 lb. bombs, were the main force. The bombing needed to be extremely accurate to achieve the desired result; Squadron Leader Rupert Oakley of 627 Squadron flew the length of the canal's defences at extremely low level to place his markers accurately. He remembers it 'being a little hot at the time'. The main force once again bombed with impeccable accuracy, the canal breached and over ten miles of the canal were drained. The Ruhr waterways were cut off from the North Sea and Berlin; over 4,000 workers were needed to rebuild both banks for a distance of two miles. For six months Bomber Command denied the enemy its most important gateway for transporting stores, coal, iron ore, etc. to and from the Ruhr. When the repairs were completed Bomber Command returned and breached the canal again! The 8th Air Force never, at any time, matched this kind of accuracy. It should be remembered that this attack, and many other similar attacks of such precision, were carried out by Bomber Command at night.

Oil targets were the first priority in 1945 but demands fell on Bomber Command from the Army commanders; some of these demands were for the destruction of cities, not only to cause industrial damage, but also to create chaos in those areas which the British, American and Russian armies were about to overrun. These attacks were to be the subject of much controversy and criticism; and it was Harris who was the man held responsible by the public at large. Harris has, in fact, been made the scapegoat for the decisions of the Chiefs of Staff and their political masters. It is necessary to study the background to these attacks to fully understand what happened in 1945.

By January, 1945, the Allied leaders had realised that the

war was far from won: General Eisenhower and the Russian commanders, in fact, considered that once the Allied armies began to fight inside Germany itself, the battles would be fierce. Eisenhower and his staff, the British and American Chiefs of Staff and the Russian Chiefs of Staff and their commanding generals now began to discuss ways and means to achieve a speedy victory, and minimise casualties in the final battles on German soil. It was agreed that air power was the key to achieving this.

The difficulty was that there was no agreement on how best to employ the Allied air power. Spaatz, the commanding general of USAAF in Europe, wanted the Luftwaffe, and its production and operational establishments, to be the primary objective. The Admiralty still wanted priority to be given to attacks on submarine production facilities. The Chief of Air Staff, Portal, considered that the first priority should be given to oil and communications. He considered that this would give the most assistance to the Russian advance, as well as to the American and British armies. The Deputy Chief of Air Staff, Bottomley, supported Portal's ideas on oil, but put forward the idea, first discussed in September 1944, of a massive sustained assault on Berlin. The American commander, Spaatz, virtually ignored Portal's ideas of attacking oil and communications and directed his subordinate commanders to concentrate their attacks on the production facilities of the new German jet aircraft.

During January 1945, Bottomley's idea of a massive assault on Berlin received support from the joint Intelligence Committee. It was the view of this Committee that a massive assault on Berlin would not, in itself, bring about a collapse of German resistance but, considered in relation to the Eastern Front, the committee believed that a massive flow of refugees from Berlin, together with the civilian refugees fleeing westward from the advancing Russian armies, would be bound to 'create great confusion, interfere with the orderly movement of troops to the front, and hamper the

German military and administrative machine'.

At this point Prime Minister Churchill entered the scene. As he prepared to leave for the Yalta Conference, where he would be meeting Stalin and Roosevelt, the Prime Minister wanted to know what evidence he could offer the Russians of Western air support for their offensive in the East.

Churchill discussed this with Sir Archibald Sinclair, the Secretary of State for Air, who in turn took the matter up with Portal. Following his consultation with Portal, Sir Archibald Sinclair wrote a long minute to the Prime Minister which ended by saying:

'Opportunities might be used to exploit the present situation by the bombing of Berlin and other large cities in Eastern Germany such as Leipzig, Dresden and Chemnitz which are not only administrative centres controlling the civilian and military movements but are also the main communication centres through which the bulk of the traffic moves ... The possibility of these attacks being delivered on the scale necessary to have critical effect on the situation in Eastern Germany is now under examination.'

Churchill sent back a peremptory minute to Sinclair which said:

'I did not ask you last night about plans for harrying the German retreat from Breslau. On the contrary, I asked whether Berlin, and no doubt other large cities in East Germany, should not now be considered especially attractive targets. I am glad that this is "under examination". Pray report to me tomorrow what is going to be done.'

On 27 January, Bottomley sent a formal instruction to Harris to carry out:

'One big attack on Berlin and related attacks on Dresden, Leipzig, Chemnitz or any other cities where a severe blitz will not only cause confusion in the evacuation from the East but will also hamper the movement of troops from the West ... as soon as moon and weather conditions allow you will undertake such attacks with the particular object of exploiting the confused conditions which are likely to exist in the above-mentioned cities during the successful Russian advance.'

On 4 February at the Yalta Conference the Russians submitted a memorandum in which they formally requested air attacks against Germany's eastern communications. On 6 February, Portal signalled Bottomley that proposals for the air attacks had been approved by the Chiefs of Staff; Harris had already received a formal directive from Bottomley, in the letter dated 27 January 1945, to carry out these attacks.

What is quite clear is that the decision to attack Dresden, Chemnitz, Leipzig and Berlin by the combined forces of Bomber Command and the United States Strategic Air Forces was not a personal decision taken by Sir Arthur Harris. In fact, Harris had not the authority to make such a decision. The bombing of these targets was the decision of the United States, Russian and British Chiefs of Staff; strongly urged upon them by Prime Minister Churchill and fully supported by Roosevelt and Stalin.

The decision received support from General Eisenhower, who made known to Churchill and Stalin his intention, after isolating the Ruhr, of making his main thrust from the West along the axis Berlin–Leipzig–Dresden.

In ordering the bombing of the Eastern German cities, the Chiefs of Staff and their political masters were asking the Allied bomber forces to support the Allied armies in order to achieve victory as swiftly as possible and with a minimum of losses. The bombers were to be used as long-range artillery, just as they had been in Normandy, but this time the targets were to be German cities.

Harris was sent his instructions to bomb Dresden, Leipzig and Chemnitz on 27 January, but he did not attack Dresden until the night of 13/14 February, and Chemnitz on the night of 14/15 February. Before attacking he contacted Bottomley at Air Ministry, and sought confirmation that he was, in fact, correct in carrying out these attacks. He was instructed to go ahead.

804 Bomber Command aircraft were despatched to attack Dresden; of these 786 claimed to have attacked the city. The attack was a 'split' raid, carried out in two stages. There was cloud over Dresden for the first stage of the attack, but this cleared for about 10 miles from the target for the second stage of the attack. It was apparent to the crews that considerable damage was caused, but photographs taken on the morning of 15 February were of poor quality; smoke from the fires still burning in the city obscured much of the area, but what was visible indicated that there had been considerable devastation.

At this point it is important to make quite clear that to Harris and the staff at Bomber Command Headquarters, who planned the attack, the Dresden operation was no different to scores of other heavy attacks mounted against Germany. The Command's attacks had by now reached an extraordinary degree of technical efficiency; there was no possible way, however, that the staff at High Wycombe could anticipate the terrible 'firestorm' which swept through Dresden causing such great devastation and the thousands of deaths in the city.

The American 8th Air Force attacked Dresden with 316 aircraft on the morning of 14 February; again on 15 February the 8th Air Force despatched 211 bombers against the city, and finally, on 2 March, the 8th attacked again with 406 bombers. The 8th Air Force carried out a further attack on Dresden on 7 April with 572 bombers.

Berlin, which had been attacked heavily by the 8th Air Force earlier in the month, was raided by Bomber Command on the night of 24 February; on 26 February the 8th Air Force assaulted Berlin with over 1,000 bombers.

As news began to reach Britain and the United States of the devastation in Dresden, concern mounted and dismay began to spread through Whitehall. The concern was increased by an Associated Press release, in which a correspondent reported that 'Allied Air Chiefs' had 'embarked on deliberate terror-bombing of German population centres as a ruthless expedient to hasten doom'. This dispatch was hastily suppressed by the censor in Britain, but it had already reached America where it caused major public controversy.

This outcry was soon echoed in Britain and questions were asked in Parliament. The controversy marked the moment when far-sighted politicians and airmen began to perceive that history might judge the bombing with less enthusiasm than it had been received with by the Allied army commanders.

General Marshall stated publicly in America that the bombing of Dresden had been carried out at the specific request of the Russians. General Arnold cabled Spaatz, seeking to be informed of the distinction between morale bombing and radar attacks on transportation targets in urban areas. Spaatz replied that 'he had not departed from the historic American policy in Europe, even in the case of Berlin,' and Arnold expressed himself as entirely satisfied with the explanation. This, of course, was another instance of hypocritical cant; its inclusion in the American History and its incessant repetition by American writers did much, however, to spare Spaatz, Eaker and Doolittle from the vilification heaped upon Sir Arthur Harris in post-war years.

Prime Minister Churchill also appeared to decide it was time to distance himself from the bombing of Dresden and, on 28 March, he sent a quite amazing minute to the Chief of Staffs Committee and the Chief of Air Staff:

'It seems to me that the moment has come when the question of bombing of German cities simply for the sake of increasing the terror, though under other pretexts, should be reviewed. Otherwise we shall come into control of an utterly ruined land. We shall not, for instance, be able to get housing materials out of Germany for our own needs because some temporary provision would have to be made for the Germans themselves. The destruction of Dresden remains a serious query against the conduct of Allied bombing. I am of the opinion that military objectives must henceforward be more strictly studied in our own interests rather than that of the enemy.'

'The Foreign Secretary has spoken to me on this subject, and I feel the need for more precise concentration upon military objectives, such as oil and communications behind the immediate battle-zone, rather than on mere acts of terror and wanton destruction, however impressive.'

This minute can only be regarded in one way, a deliberate and calculated attempt by the Prime Minister to distance himself from the bombing of Dresden, and the rising controversy surrounding area bombing, and to place on record for posterity a written statement of his objections to the bombing.

It was a quite astonishing memorandum: Churchill had been the greatest advocate for destroying Germany city by city and in late January, before his departure for Yalta, had been pressing for Bomber Command attacks against Eastern German cities, including Dresden.

Portal was angered by the Prime Minister's minute and instructed his deputy, Bottomley, to immediately ask for Harris's comments. It is not known whether Harris ever saw the actual minute, but on 28 March, Bottomley wrote to Harris a personal and confidential letter, putting all the points Churchill had made in the minute and asking for Harris's comments as a matter of urgency.

An outraged Sir Arthur Harris replied promptly and pungently; he was infuriated, and with good reason. The full text of Harris's letter is printed in Appendix Three of this book, it is a fascinating letter and fully reveals Sir Arthur's anger and his personal feelings.

At the Chiefs of Staff committee meeting on 30 March, an angry Portal backed by the letter from Sir Arthur Harris made his feelings known; Churchill withdrew his original minute and substituted the following:

'It seems to me that the moment has come when the

question of the so-called "area bombing" of German cities should be reviewed from the point of view of our own interests. If we come into control of an entirely ruined land, there will be a great shortage of accommodation for ourselves and our Allies: and we shall be unable to get housing materials out of Germany for our own needs because some temporary provision would have to be made for the Germans themselves. We must see to it that our attacks do not do more harm to ourselves in the long run than they do to the enemy's immediate war effort. Pray let me have your views.'

Everything written above is a matter of public record, and can easily be verified by anyone who cares to take the time and trouble to research the matter thoroughly. Despite this, ever since the war years, Sir Arthur Harris has been the subject of vilification and denigration by journalists, television producers and some writers who call themselves 'historians'. In recent years books have appeared by journalists and novelists which have been merely sensation-seeking diatribes of the 'sneer and smear' variety. As a result, in the public's mind, Sir Arthur Harris has been identified as the 'Man who ordered the bombing of Dresden.'

On Thursday 5 April, 1984, the day Sir Arthur Harris died, Independent Television News opened its main programme with the words, 'The man who ordered the bombing of Dresden is dead'. This sentence was repeated in the popular press the following day.

The American Official History has been largely responsible for the post-war generations believing that it was only Harris and Bomber Command who were responsible for the area bombing of German cities. The truth is the American commanders matched Harris ruin for ruin over Germany. Spaatz was perfectly willing to commit his bomber force to bombing cities, but always some window dressing was provided such as 'blind bombing of transportation centres'. Other airmen, both British and American – Tedder, Slessor and Eaker prominent among them, prevaricated about their participation in area bombing. General Eaker in a letter to Spaatz dated 1 January 1945 and quoted by the American Historians, said, 'We should never allow the history of this war to convict us of throwing the strategic bomber at the man in the street'.

In all the abuse hurled at Harris and Bomber Command over the Dresden attack it seems to have been forgotten that the USAAF also played its part in the attack on the city. The vast American fire-raising attacks on Japan by General Curtis Lemay's B29 Super Fortresses, in which 84,000 people were killed in one day, have also escaped censure. These attacks, with their dreadful casualties, were carried out before the atomic bomb had been heard of.

It has been Sir Arthur Harris who has received the censure of the post-war generations; unfairly so, while politicians and military commanders who bore far more responsibility for the bombing of Dresden. In fact, for the bombing policy as a whole they have escaped the vilification hurled upon Harris.

In a way Sir Arthur Harris could be said to be partly responsible for this himself: while politicians, generals and other airmen sought prudent cover Sir Arthur never did, nor did he make any excuse or apology for what his force had done during the war years. Over the years Sir Arthur Harris never entered into public controversy over Bomber Command's part in the Second World War and on only one occasion did he deign to answer criticism. Attlee, the Deputy Prime Minister to Churchill, publicly said that Bomber Command should not have devoted so much effort to attacking German cities. Harris reminded Attlee that he had been one of the leading members of the War Cabinet, and as such had been largely responsible for formulating the bombing policy which Harris had executed.

Sir Arthur Harris's attitude to his critics during the post-war years had been typical of this great commander's 'bigness' of character – 'They can say what they like about me, but I get angry when they attempt to denigrate my magnificent aircrews'.

CHAPTER FIFTEEN

The Chiefs of Staff formally decreed the ending of the area bombing campaign on 16 April, 1945; but Bomber Command did not wait out the last weeks of war in idleness.

The Command's aircraft bombed some of the remaining oil plants, the coastal guns on Wangerooge and Hitler's stronghold at Berchtesgaden. One of the last operations of the war was against the German island fortress of Heligoland, where German naval radar had first detected Wing Commander Kellett's Wellington formation before the air battle on 18 December 1939. The last attack of the war was on the night of 2/3 May, 1945, when 125 Mosquitoes attacked the port of Kiel. The Mosquitoes bombed in two waves using OBOE; the bombing was extremely accurate, and the official comment on the opposition was 'Defences Nil'.

During the Second World War Sir Arthur Harris and his bomber crews had been heroes to the British people; but soon after the fighting stopped there was a subtle change in attitude. Harris failed to be recognised in the distribution of post-war honours; and something that hurt Harris badly, his request for a campaign medal for the personnel of Bomber Command was refused. Harris commented bitterly at the time that his personnel were to receive 'only a Home Defence medal whilst every clerk, butcher, baker and candlestick maker, serving miles behind the fighting fronts on the Continent, in Egypt and the East was to get a campaign medal'. Harris wrote to Portal pointing out the casualties among his ground crews, let alone his aircrews, and the awful conditions in which the ground crews had toiled through the years of the bombing campaign; he concluded his letter in typical manner:

'I must tell you here and now ... that if my Command are

to have the Defence Medal and no Campaign Medal … then I, too, will have the Defence Medal and no other…. I will be proud indeed to wear the Defence Medal and that alone … and as bitter as the rest of my personnel.'

The refusal of a Campaign Medal to the air and ground personnel of Bomber Command was a particularly petty act on the part of the Government. The Command had fought a long and bitter campaign lasting almost exactly five and a half years. In one night alone; 30/31 March 1944, the night of the attack on Nuremberg, 545 bomber aircrew men had died, as compared with the total number of deaths of 507 during the Battle of Britain. During the post-war years it would be the pilots of Fighter Command who would receive the acclaim and adulation of the people of Britain. No-one would wish to deprecate the valiant part played by Fighter Command, but why had the politicians and public turned away from the men and women of Bomber Command?

The new Labour Government had little time for the man who had carried out the now embarrassing area bombing policy and Harris was ignored in the post-war Victory Honours List.

All the other victorious commanders were honoured: the three Chiefs of Staff were made Viscounts; so also were Field Marshal Alexander and Field Marshal Montgomery. Admiral Fraser, Field Marshal Wilson and Marshal of the Royal Air Force Tedder were created Barons; but Sir Arthur Harris was snubbed.

No sooner had the Labour Government indicated its indifference to the contribution that Harris and Bomber Command had made to the war, than Harris began to come under attack. Left wing politicians and intellectuals condemned the bombing policy and the attacks on cities; sorrow for the German people seemed to pervade their minds, they appeared to have no thought for the disaster that would have befallen Britain if the bombing offensive had not been so effective. They had apparently forgotten the more than 6,000,000 Jewish men, women and children who had died in the extermination camps.

They had apparently also forgotten that the war had been fought under a National Coalition Government, in which the leader of their own party had been Deputy Prime Minister, and in which the Labour Party had been well represented at Cabinet level. The Labour Party members of the War Cabinet held more responsibility for the area bombing policy than did Sir Arthur Harris; he was merely the commander in the field who executed the policy laid down by those above him.

It appeared that the Labour Government wished to turn its head away from the bombing of Germany; Harris, the man who had carried out the bombing policy, was an embarrassment, and he retired unhonoured from the Royal Air Force. It was not until eight years later, when Churchill was again Prime Minister, that Harris became a Baronet.

Whilst this book was in preparation the authorised biography of Sir Arthur Harris was published. This book, written by one of Harris's former staff officers, Group Captain Dudley Saward, was written some years ago, but Harris refused to allow publication until after his death. Dudley Saward was privileged to have access to Harris's private papers, together with many long interviews with Harris. The biography is an excellent book, and contains much revealing information which has hitherto not been available. It reveals that the reason for the treatment of Harris could possibly have been a personal vendetta against him by a member of the Labour Government. It is a fascinating book which does justice to this great man; one of the few that has done so, and anyone wishing to study the character of Sir Arthur Harris should certainly read it.

Much has been written since the war about Sir Arthur Harris and Bomber Command. Most of the criticism levelled against Bomber Command and its commander has been based on a writer's own aversion to bombing; some of the criticism has been due to ignorance or because the writer has been ill-informed and has not thoroughly researched his subject.

Much of the criticism has been based on the Official

History *The Strategic Air Offensive Against Germany*. The History frequently in an indirect, veiled manner; but often in a direct and more immediate way; attacks Harris's views on strategic bombing, his handling of the bomber force, and says that much of the bomber effort was wasted.

The choice of the historians was strange indeed. The late Sir Charles Webster, Emeritus Professor of International History at the University of London, was appointed to write the history. Chosen to assist him was Dr Noble Frankland, an ex-Bomber Command navigator and holder of the DFC.

Webster had already made it clear that he was violently opposed to the bomber offensive. His choice was therefore a curious one. In November 1952 Webster visited Harris but, according to Harris, made no move to seek his co-operation and showed a complete indifference to Harris's views.

In November 1958, Webster wrote to Harris advising him that the draft of the History was complete and asking whether Harris would like to look at the draft and comment 'unofficially'. Harris replied to the effect that, since he had received no official request to assist with the History, he found it odd that he should be asked to comment 'unofficially' and that he wished to have nothing to do with it.

Portal also refused to have anything to do with the History, but when two particularly offensive passages were drawn to his attention he did insist that Webster delete them.

The historians had access to all official documents, but it does not appear that they interviewed such people as Albert Speer, Hitler's Armaments Minister; neither do they appear to have met and talked with members of Germany's armed forces, or studied Swiss intelligence reports.

Many ex-Bomber Command aircrew find much with which to disagree strongly in the History; a lot of the History is coloured by Webster's own aversion to bombing. Even so, those writers who have used the History to support their criticism of Harris rarely quote some passages which even Webster could not fail to include in his balance sheet:

'The fact is that had Germany not been devastated with

fire and high explosive, and had not her industries in the process melted away, she must have won the war. For she would inevitably have been able to build a bomber fleet and to have wrought far greater destruction than she in fact achieved. In that case what happened in Coventry would soon have been wiped from public memory by far greater and more devastating holocausts. That she would have done so without scruple or pity can reasonably be inferred from the action taken by the Luftwaffe in the days of its strength against Warsaw, Rotterdam and Belgrade, and for that matter against London.

'In turning the weapon of air war against her, therefore, the pilots and crews of Bomber Command were as much the saviours of their country as were the pilots of Fighter Command in the Battle of Britain.'

The History also concludes that:

'Both cumulatively in largely indirect ways and eventually in a more immediate and direct manner, strategic bombing and also, in other roles, strategic bombers, made a contribution to victory which was decisive.'

Could the offensive have been handled better? Of course it could, especially in the earlier days of the war; but after Harris took command the Command was revitalised. From 1942 to the end of the war Harris fought his campaign with a single-mindedness and determination that were the attributes of a truly great commander. Surely, no-one can really question the high ideals of this man who tried so hard to defeat Germany without the terrible carnage of a prolonged land campaign similar to that of 1914–18.

Yet three days after Harris died the *Daily Express* carried a particularly vicious attack on him written by the journalist George Gale, in which Gale compared Harris with the Nazi war criminals. The article was disgraceful and did no credit to Gale or his paper. A certain Royal Personage once described the *Daily Express* as a 'Bloody awful newspaper.' If Gale's attack on Harris is the standard of journalism to which the paper aspires, then that description would appear to be an accurate one.

One wonders whether Mr Gale remembers 1940–1941: Britain was without an ally in the world other than her own distant Empire. Bomber Command was the only weapon with which this country could strike against the enemy.

Germany had overrun most of Europe, the Nazis were systematically exterminating the Jewish race; all Slavic peoples had been declared sub-humans by the Nazis. The Gestapo was terrifying and torturing throughout Occupied Europe and countless numbers of innocent men and women had been taken from their homes to work in Germany as slaves. It should never be forgotten that if Nazi Germany had defeated Britain then that would have been the plan for the occupation of this country; the people of Britain would have been a nation of slaves to a barbaric conqueror.

The wartime actions of Bomber Command and its Commander in Chief cannot, and should not, be judged out of the context of the period.

It is to the discredit of the people of Britain that Sir Arthur Harris, one of this country's great military commanders, never received the recognition that is his rightful due.

It is perhaps significant that, right up to the end of the war, the British Government attempted to conceal from the British people, and the world at large, that Sir Arthur Harris and Bomber Command had been expressly ordered by the Government to undertake the area bombing of Germany. Sir Archibald Sinclair, the Secretary of State of Air, repeatedly said in Parliament that Bomber Command was attacking purely military objectives: throughout the war the British press and radio had made the same claim. If civilians had been killed, or if historic buildings and works of art had been destroyed, then that was purely accidental; according to the politicians and the media.

After the war, with thousands of British Servicemen stationed in Germany, the devastation and ruin of Germany and the true nature of area bombing became gradually known to the British public. The press, which had helped the

Government conceal the facts, now became critical of the Command. Strangely, it was not the politicians who had laid down the policy and given the orders who came in for media criticism and public hostility, but the Commander in Chief of Bomber Command. The public appeared to believe that Harris was the sole devisor, controller and commander of the bombing campaign; not just the commander in the field whose sole authority was to devise and control the tactics of the bomber force in accordance with the orders he was given from those in authority above him.

As press criticism grew and public distaste grew stronger, Harris remained unrepentant, he pointed out that all war is inhumane and an act of idiocy. He also pointed out that the bombing of Germany had undoubtedly saved the lives of thousands of Allied soldiers. Another point he made strongly was that bombing of Germany had caused less deaths among the civilian population than the British naval blockade of the First World War, when an estimated eight hundred thousand Germans – mainly women, children and old people – had died. These facts fell on deaf ears, however, and public criticism of the bombing grew; this may have been another reason why Sir Arthur Harris was a convenient scapegoat. In appearing to hold Harris solely responsible for the destruction of German cities, and the deaths of German civilians, the politicians were able to turn the public disquiet away from themselves and onto the head of Harris.

After Sir Arthur Harris retired from the Royal Air Force, unrewarded and unhonoured for his service to his country, he wrote his memoirs. His book *Bomber Offensive* is a model of what a military commander's memoirs should be. In it Harris makes no apology or excuse for anything Bomber Command did over Germany whilst he was Commander in Chief; nor should anyone expect him to have done.

During his period of command, Harris fought over 1,000 battles; for that is what the Command's attacks on Germany were. Often, sometimes several times a week, he committed his entire front-line force to battle. There were occasions when he had to commit all of his reserve strength as well. Few, if any, commanders have ever fought so varied and difficult a campaign. Each time he committed his force to battle he had to take a calculated risk, not only with the enemy but also with the weather; no-one knew better than he that any one of these operations could turn into disaster. Harris has been criticised by some for the losses on the Nuremberg operation; those who make this criticism are ignorant of the realities of the risks inherent in every operation the Command mounted. As Harris himself has commented; it is surprising there were not more Nurembergs.

It was Harris's courage, single-mindedness and determination that drove him to demand the utmost of his aircrews, not once but time and time again. Yet at the same time as he demanded the utmost of his crews, he strove his utmost to do all he could on their behalf. Harris was criticised by some people, so called 'experts', for not attacking what they considered 'desirable' targets. However, it was because he refused to use his crews for purposes for which he considered they were untrained, or on targets which he considered were not worth the needless loss of his men's lives for little or no result, that he vigorously opposed these 'experts' proposals.

The politicians and the public may have turned away from Sir Arthur Harris but there were, and are, few men and women who served under Harris's command who do not feel proud to have done so.

Many of the men and women who served in Bomber Command, particularly the surviving aircrew men, were hurt when their actions were later declared by some critics to be unworthy. They should not be made to feel this way: Sir Arthur Harris and the men and women of Bomber Command fought with the highest ideals against an evil and barbaric regime.

The survivors of Bomber Command have no reason to feel other than great pride in their service to their country in the years 1939 to 1945.

EPILOGUE

During the Second World War Bomber Command despatched 364,514 bombing and leaflet-dropping sorties: from these operations a total of 8,325 aircraft failed to return. This was a loss rate of 2·28 per cent, this figure does not include the mining and secret operations undertaken by the Command. Figures are not available for these operations but it is probable that a further 300 plus were lost on them. It is believed that a further 1,500 plus aircraft were written off following severe battle damage or crashes in Britain.

Of the 72,786 killed and 6,538 missing of the Royal Air Force during World War Two; 55,573 were from Bomber Command alone. This figure includes the dead of the Dominion and Allied Forces who flew in Bomber Command, but it does not include the thousands who, after parachuting from their crippled bombers, became prisoners of war. Nor does it include those crews who were killed in accidents, or those who were wounded by enemy action or in aircraft crashes: many of these men were permanently disabled.

The total number of aircrew who flew operationally with Bomber Command from 1939 to 1945 was just over 110,000; the casualty figures were the highest sustained by any arm of Britain's fighting services during World War Two.

A further 1,363 male ground staff and 91 WAAFs also died while serving with Bomber Command, and the sacrifice made by these men and women should never be forgotten.

On 9 June 1984, I drove to the town of Selby in Yorkshire. It is forty years since I was last in Selby. I was then a young RAF officer. I would not have returned this time, but for a very special reason.

On 9 June a memorial was unveiled in the grounds of Selby Abbey; a memorial to the aircrews who lost their lives while serving with 51 Squadron. Almost 500 people, including surviving members of the squadron, widows, families and local civic dignitaries packed the beautiful old Abbey for a service of thanksgiving: thanksgiving for the men who gave their lives flying with 51 Squadron. The service was simple, dignified and moving. After the service the congregation moved into the Abbey grounds for the unveiling of the memorial; a simple granite stone which will now stand in the Abbey grounds as a permanent memorial to those young men who died flying with the squadron in the service of their country.

The memorial was paid for by donations from members of 51 Squadron Association; the first wreath to be laid after its dedication was that of the Association. Other wreaths were laid by the present commander of the Squadron and the chairman of Selby District Council. As the memorial was unveiled a tribute to the fallen comrades was paid by the present Squadron when a lone Nimrod aircraft flew low over the assembled congregation.

I am not normally an emotional man, but as I looked around at the assembled throng, the widows so proudly wearing their husbands' decorations, my friends and comrades come to honour those who did not survive, and the Squadron Standard with its escort of present Squadron members, I was moved to tears.

It is fitting that this memorial should stand in the grounds of the Abbey: Selby was 'home' to 51 Squadron during its time at RAF Snaith. The last 'home' that so many young men knew: the casualties on this one small unit were indeed heavy.

During the years 1939 to 1945 No.51 Squadron's losses were:

52 Whitley aircraft
128 Halifax aircraft

A total of 980 men lost their lives whilst serving with the squadron during the Second World War.

We will remember them

APPENDIX ONE
SPECIFICATION OF PRINCIPAL AIRCRAFT
OF BOMBER COMMAND 1939–1945

It is impossible to detail all the different Marks of each aircraft. Those chosen relate most closely to the events described in the text. Performance figures can only be an approximate guide, since individual aircraft varied immensely in efficiency and handling. In the later stages of the campaign some Lancasters, for instance, were modified to carry a bombload of ten tons.

Vickers WELLINGTON IC
Type: Twin-engined medium bomber. Crew: Six. Engines: Pegasus 18. Dimensions: Length–60·8 feet, wingspan–86 feet, height–18·75 feet. Maximum loaded weight: 30,000 lb. Armament: Twin ·303 machine-guns in front and rear turrets, single free ·303s on beam mountings. Bombload: 4,500 lb. (with fuel for 1,200 miles)/1,000 lb. (with fuel for 2,550 miles). Ceiling: 15,000 feet. Maximum speed: 235 mph. Cruising speed: 165 mph.

Bristol BLENHEIM I V
Type: Twin-engined light bomber. Crew: Three. Engines: Mercury 15. Dimensions: Length–40 feet, wingspan–56 feet, height–9·2 feet. Maximum loaded weight: 15,800 lb. Armament: Twin ·303s in forward under nacelle, single ·303 in rear turret, single ·303 rearward fixed firing from engine nacelle. Bombload: 1,000 lb. (with fuel for 1,460 miles). Ceiling 22,000 feet. Maximum speed: 266 mph. Cruising speed: 180 mph.

Armstrong Whitworth WHITLEY V
Type: Twin-engined medium bomber. Crew: Five. Engines: Merlin X. Dimensions: Length–69·3 feet,

wingspan–84 feet, height–12·75 feet. Maximum loaded weight: 33,500 lb. Armament: Single free ·303 in forward turret, four ·303s in rear turret. Bombload: 8,000 lb. (with fuel for 630 miles)/3,500 lb. (with fuel for 1,930 miles). Ceiling: 17,600 feet. Maximum speed: 202 mph. Cruising speed: 165 mph.

Handley Page HAMPDEN

Type: Twin-engined medium bomber. Crew: Four. Engines: Pegasus 18. Dimensions: length–53.3 feet, wingspan–69·3 feet, height–14·9 feet. Maximum loaded weight: 22,500 lb. Armament: Single fixed and single free ·303 in nose, single or twin free ·303s in rear and mid-under positions. Bombload: 4,000 lb. (with fuel for 1,200 miles)/2,000 lb. (with fuel for 1,885 miles). Ceiling: 20,000 feet. Maximum speed: 243 mph. Cruising speed: 155 mph.

Avro MANCHESTER

Type: Twin-engined heavy-medium bomber. Crew: Seven. Maximum loaded weight: 50,000 lb. Engines: Vulture 2. Dimensions: Length–68·8 feet, wingspan–90·1 feet, height–19·5 feet. Armament: Twin ·303s in front and mid-upper turrets, four ·303s in rear turret. Bombload: 10,350 lb. (with fuel for 1,200 miles)/8,100 lb. (with fuel for 1,630 miles). Ceiling: 19,200 feet. Maximum speed: 258 mph. Cruising speed: 185 mph.

Short STIRLING III

Type: Four-engined heavy bomber. Crew: Seven. Engines: Hercules Sixteen. Dimensions: Length–87 feet, wingspan–99 feet, height–22·75 feet. Maximum loaded weight: 70,000 lb. Armament: Twin ·303s in front and mid-upper turrets, four ·303s in rear turret. Bombload: 14,000 lb. (with fuel for 590 miles)/2,010 lb. (with fuel for 3,575 miles). Ceiling: 17,000 feet. Maximum speed: 270 mph. Cruising speed: 200 mph.

Handley Page HALIFAX Mk .III

Type: Four-engined heavy bomber. Crew: Seven. Engines: Hercules Sixteen. Dimensions: Length–70·1 feet, wingspan–104 feet, height–20·75 feet. Maximum loaded weight: 65,000 lb. Armament: Single ·303 in nose, four ·303s in mid-upper turret, four ·303s in rear turret. Bombload: 13,000 lb. (with fuel for 980 miles)/6,250 lb. (with fuel for 2,005 miles). Ceiling: 22,000 feet. Maximum speed: 281 mph. Cruising speed: 225 mph.

Avro LANCASTER Mk. I and Mk. III

Type: Four-engined heavy bomber. Crew: Seven. Engines: Merlin 22, 28 or 38. Dimensions: Length–69·6 feet, wingspan–102 feet, height–20·6 feet. Maximum loaded weight: 68,000 lb. Armament: Twin ·303s in front and mid-upper turrets, four ·303s in rear turret. Bombload: 14,000 lb. (with fuel for 1,660 miles). Ceiling: 24,500 feet. Maximum speed: 287 mph. Cruising speed: 216 mph.

De Havilland MOSQUITO Mk. IV

Type: Twin-engined light bomber and Pathfinder marker aircraft. Crew: Two. Engines: Merlin 21 or 23. Dimensions: Length–40·8 feet, wingspan–54·2 feet, height–15·3 feet. Maximum loaded weight 21,462 lb. Armament: Nil. Bombload: 2,000 lb. (with fuel for 1,620 miles). Some aircraft were modified to carry a 4,000 lb. bomb. Ceiling: 33,000 feet. Maximum speed: 380 mph. Cruising speed: 265 mph.

APPENDIX TWO
RAF BOMBER COMMAND
ORDER OF BATTLE AS AT 1st APRIL 1944

1 GROUP
(Air Vice-Marshal E.A.B. Rice)
HQ Bawtry Hall

Squadron	Station	Aircraft
12	Wickenby	Lancaster
100	Grimsby	Lancaster
101	Ludford Magna	Lancaster (ABC Equipped)
103	Elsham Wolds	Lancaster
166	Kirmington	Lancaster
300 (Polish)	Faldingworth	Wellington/Lancaster
460 (RAAF)	Binbrook	Lancaster
550	North Killingholme	Lancaster
576	Elsham Wolds	Lancaster
625	Kelstern	Lancaster
626	Wickenby	Lancaster

3 GROUP
(Air Vice-Marshal R. Harrison)
HQ Exning Newmarket

Squadron	Station	Aircraft
15	Mildenhall	Lancaster
75 (New Zealand)	Mepal	Stirling/Lancaster
90	Tuddenham	Stirling
115	Witchford	Lancaster
149 (East India)	Lakenheath	Stirling
199	Lakenheath	Stirling
218 (Gold Coast)	Woolfox Lodge	Stirling/Lancaster
514	Waterbeach	Lancaster
622	Mildenhall	Lancaster

Secret Operations Squadrons

Squadron	Station	Aircraft
138	Tempsford	Halifax, Liberator, Hudson
161	Tempsford	and Lysander

4 GROUP
(Air Vice-Marshal C.R. Carr)
HQ Heslington Hall, York

Squadron	Station	Aircraft
10	Melbourne	Halifax
51	Snaith	Halifax
76	Holme-on-Spalding-Moor	Halifax
77	Elvington	Halifax
78	Breighton	Halifax
102 (Ceylon)	Pocklington	Halifax
158	Lissett	Halifax
466 (RAAF)	Leconfield	Halifax
578	Burn	Halifax
640	Leconfield	Halifax

5 GROUP
(Air Vice-Marshal the Hon. Ralph Cochrane)
HQ Morton Hall, Swinderby

Squadron	Station	Aircraft
9	Bardney	Lancaster
44 (Rhodesia)	Dunholme Lodge	Lancaster
49	Fiskerton	Lancaster
50	Skellingthorpe	Lancaster
57	East Kirkby	Lancaster
61	Coningsby	Lancaster
106	Metheringham	Lancaster
207	Spilsby	Lancaster
463 (RAAF)	Waddington	Lancaster
467 (RAAF)	Waddington	Lancaster
617	Woodhall Spa	Lancaster
619	Coningsby	Lancaster
630	East Kirkby	Lancaster

6 (CANADIAN) GROUP
(Air Vice-Marshal C.M. McEwen)
HQ Allerton Park Castle, Knaresborough

Squadron	Station	Aircraft
408 (Goose)	Linton-on-Ouse	Lancaster
419 (Moose)	Middleton St. George	Halifax/Lancaster
420 (Snowy Owl)	Tholthorpe	Halifax
424 (Tiger)	Skipton-on-Swale	Halifax
425 (Alouette)	Tholthorpe	Halifax
426 (Thunderbird)	Linton-on-Ouse	Lancaster
427 (Lion)	Leeming	Halifax
428 (Ghost)	Middleton St. George	Halifax
429 (Bison)	Leeming	Halifax
431 (Iroquois)	Croft	Halifax
432 (Leaside)	East Moor	Halifax
433 (Porcupine)	Skipton-on-Swale	Halifax
434 (Bluenose)	Croft Halifax	

8 (Pathfinder Force) GROUP
(Air Vice-Marshal D.C.T. Bennett)
HQ Castle Hill House, Huntingdon

Squadron	Station	Aircraft
7	Oakington Lancaster	
35 (Madras Presidency)	Graveley	Lancaster
83	Wyton	Lancaster
97 (Straits Settlements)	Bourn	Lancaster
105	Bourn	Mosquito (OBOE Equipped)
109	Marham	Mosquito (OBOE Equipped)
139 (Jamaica)	Upwood	Mosquito
156	Upwood	Lancaster
405 (Vancouver)RCAF	Gransden Lodge	Lancaster
627	Oakington	Mosquito
635	Downham Market	Lancaster
692 (Fellowship of the Bellows)		
	Graveley	Mosquito
1409 (Meteorological)		
Flight	Wyton	Mosquito

100 (BOMBER SUPPORT) GROUP
(Air Commodore E.B. Addison)
HQ Bylaugh Hall, East Dereham

Squadron	Station	Aircraft
141	West Raynham	Mosquito
169	Little Snoring	Mosquito
192	Foulsham	Halifax, Wellington and Mosquito
214 (Federated Malay States)		
	Sculthorpe	B 17 Flying Fortress
239	West Raynham	Mosquito
515	Little Snoring	Mosquito

APPENDIX THREE

Letter from Sir Arthur Harris to Sir Norman Bottomley
AIR 20/3218 Headquarters, Bomber Command High
Wycombe, Bucks 29th March, 1945
ATH/DO/4B
PERSONAL AND TOP SECRET
Dear Norman,

It is difficult to answer indictments of which the terms are not fully revealed and for this reason I cannot deal as thoroughly as I should like with the points raised in your CAS608/DSAS of March 28th. I take it, however, that it is unnecessary for me to make any comment on the passages which you quote and which, without the context, are abusive in effect, though doubtless not in intention.

To suggest that we have bombed German cities 'simply for the sake of increasing the terror though under other pretexts' and to speak of our offensive as including 'mere acts of terror and wanton destruction' is an insult both to the bombing policy of the Air Ministry and to the manner in which that policy has been executed by Bomber Command. This sort of thing if it deserves an answer will certainly receive none from me, after three years of implementing official policy.

As regards the specific points raised in your letter, namely the adverse economic effects on ourselves by increasing yet further the material havoc in Germany and the destruction of Dresden in particular, the answer is surely very simple. (The feeling, such as there is, over Dresden could be easily explained by any psychiatrist. It is connected with German bands and Dresden shepherdesses. Actually Dresden was a mass of munition works, an intact government centre, and a key transportation point to the East. It is now none of those things.) It is already demonstrated in the liberated countries that what really makes any sort of recovery almost impossible is less the destruction of buildings than the complete dislocation of transportation. If, therefore, this objection is to be taken seriously I suggest that the transportation plan rather than the strategic bombing of cities is what needs to be considered, as I understand it has been, and for precisely that reason. You will remember that Dresden was recommended by the Targets Committee as a transportation target, as well as on other grounds.

I do not, however, stress this point since I assume that what is really at issue is (a) whether our strategic bombing policy up to date has been justified (b) whether the time has now come to discontinue this policy. I will therefore confine myself to these questions.

As regards (a) I have on previous occasions discussed this matter very fully in official correspondence with the Air Ministry and to avoid repetition I refer you to the following correspondence:

(i) Bomber Command letter BC/S.23801/Press/C-in-C of October 25th, 1943.

(ii) Air Ministry letter CS.21079/43 of December 15th, 1943.

(iii) Bomber Command letter BC/S.23801/Press/C-in-C of December 23rd, 1943.

(iv) Air Ministry letter CS.21079 of March 2nd, 1944.

(v) Bomber Command letter BC/S.31152/Air/C-in-C of March 7th, 1944.

I have always held and still maintain that my Directive, which you quote, 'the progressive destruction and dislocation of the German military, industrial and economic systems' could be carried out only by the elimination of German industrial cities and not merely by attacks on individual factories however important these might be in themselves. This view was also officially confirmed by the Air Ministry. The overwhelming evidence which is now available to support it makes it quite superfluous for me to argue at length that the destruction of those cities has fatally weakened the German war effort and is now enabling Allied soldiers to advance into the heart of Germany with negligible casualties. Hence the only question which I have to answer is this: would confining ourselves to more precise concentration upon military objectives such as oil and communications behind the immediate battle-zone tend to shorten the war more than persistence in attacks on cities? The answer appears to me to be obvious; but even if it is not, I must point out as I have frequently done before that we have by no means a free choice in the matter. Weather conditions frequently constrain me to decide between attacking cities and not attacking at all. When this happens it is surely evident that it is expedient to attack the cities. I can only find, pinpoint and hit small targets with a small part of my force at a time, and I have not enough fighter escort to do more than two such small attacks daily.

I have thus disposed of point (a). We have never gone in for terror bombing and the attacks which we have made in accordance with my Directive have in fact produced the strategic consequences for which they were designed and from which the Armies now profit.

Point (b) is rather difficult to follow. It can hardly mean that attacks on cities no longer produce dislocation in the German war effort. Quite the contrary is the case. The nearer Germany is to collapse the less capable she is of reorganising to meet disasters of this kind and we ought logically to make a special effort to eliminate the few cities which still remain more or less serviceable.

I therefore assume that the view under consideration is something like this; 'No doubt in the past we were justified in attacking German cities. But to do so was always repugnant and now that the Germans are beaten anyway we can properly abstain from proceeding with these attacks'. This is a doctrine to which I could never subscribe. Attacks on cities like any other act of war are intolerable unless they are strategically justified. But they are strategically justified in so far as they tend to shorten the war and so preserve the lives of Allied soldiers. To my mind we have absolutely no right to give them up unless it is certain that they will not have this effect. I do not personally regard the whole of the remaining cities of Germany as worth the bones of one British Grenadier.

It therefore seems to me that there is one, and only one, valid argument on which a case for giving up strategic bombing could be based, namely that it has already completed its task and that nothing now remains for the Armies to do except to occupy Germany against unorganised resistance. If this is what is meant I shall no doubt be informed of it. It does not however appear to be the view of the Supreme Commander. Until it is, I submit that the strategic bombing of German cities must go on.

Some final points. As you know Transportation targets are now largely off. Oil has had, and is getting, all we can practically give it in consideration of weather and escort factors. We answer every Army support call and, as Monty tells us, in a 'decisive manner'; we have asked for more but there aren't any. High Explosive is seriously limited in supply. Incendiaries are not. All these factors must therefore also be considered, and the inevitable answer is that either we continue as in the past or we very largely stand-down altogether. The last alternative would certainly be welcome. I take little delight in the work and none whatever in risking my crews avoidably.

Japan remains. Are we going to bomb their cities flat – as in Germany – and give the Armies a walk over – as in France and Germany – or going to bomb only their outlying factories (largely underground by the time we get going) and subsequently invade at the cost of 3 to 6 million casualties?

We should be careful of precedents.
   Yours ever,

Bert.

To:
Air Marshal Sir Norman Bottomley, KCB, CIE, DSO, AFC.
Air Ministry,
Whitehall. SW1.

INDEX